THE LAW IS (NOT) FOR KIDS

THE LAW IS (NOT) FOR KIDS

A LEGAL RIGHTS GUIDE FOR CANADIAN CHILDREN AND TEENS

Ned Lecic and Marvin Zuker

AU PRESS

Copyright © 2019 Ned Lecic and Marvin Zuker
Published by AU Press, Athabasca University
1200, 10011 – 109 Street, Edmonton, AB T5J 3S8

ISBN 978-1-77199-237-4 (pbk.)   ISBN 978-1-77199-238-1 (PDF)
ISBN 978-1-77199-239-8 (epub)   DOI: 10.15215/aupress/9781771992374.01

Cover images © Chelsea Victoria and Giada Canu / Stocksy.com
Cover design by Natalie Olsen, kisscutdesign.com
Interior design by Sergiy Kozakov
Printed and bound in Canada

Library and Archives Canada Cataloguing in Publication

Lecic, Ned, 1979-, author
     The law is (not) for kids : a legal rights guide for Canadian children
and teens / Ned Lecic and Marvin A. Zuker.

Includes bibliographical references.
Issued in print and electronic formats.

     1. Children—Legal status, laws, etc.—Canada. 2. Teenagers—Legal
status, laws, etc.—Canada. 3. Children's rights—Canada. 4. Parent and
child (Law)—Canada. I. Zuker, Marvin A., author II. Title.

KE512.L43 2019   342.7108'772   C2018-905821-8
KF479.C44 2019   C2018-905822-6

We acknowledge the financial support of the Government of Canada
through the Canada Book Fund (CBF) for our publishing activities and the
assistance provided by the Government of Alberta, Alberta Media Fund.

Canada   Alberta
                Government

CONTENTS

PREFACE

"Why should young people care about the law?" This is a question some of you may have as you begin reading this book. The answer is that the law defines specific rights and responsibilities that apply to young people as well as to adults. Our rights oblige other people to treat us in certain ways; our responsibilities oblige *us* to behave in certain ways. Many people are more interested in their legal rights than in their responsibilities—but the two go hand in hand. If you don't know what your legal responsibilities are, you can get into trouble. Similarly, if you don't know what your legal rights are, you won't know what to expect or what to ask for from others.

You may already have heard things from other people about rules that the law makes for you. Perhaps you're not sure exactly what these rules are, though, or perhaps you're wondering whether what they told you is really true. And even if you haven't been told anything, children and young people are often curious about questions like these:

- Are parents allowed to spank their children?
- What rules can my school make?

- Can I make any of my own decisions before I turn 18?

- If my parents get a divorce, can I decide which one I'm going to live with?

- Can my parents kick me out of the house? And if they can, how old do I have to be before they can do that?

- What can happen to me if I'm arrested?

- If I feel like I'm not being treated fairly, who can help me?

We have written this book to answer such questions, as well as a great many others. Our aim is to give you a detailed but practical guide to the laws in Canada that determine what your rights and responsibilities are and at what age a given law may apply to you. We will also tell you about what resources exist to help enforce the rights you do have and what strategies you might use to defend or enhance your rights.

We hope that, as you read, you will realize that you do have *some* rights under the law, even though those rights are still rather restricted. In some situations, you may indeed have the law on your side if you wish to make your own choices or do things that are normally thought of as adult activities. All the same, the law still usually sees young people as having only a limited ability to make sensible decisions for themselves, and so it gives adults the power to control them in numerous ways.

We also hope that we can help you steer clear of incomplete or inaccurate advice. Some people have misguided ideas about what the law actually says. They may be interested in the law, but they may not understand its rules very well, and so they can spread inaccurate information even if they don't mean to do so. For that reason, it can be risky to just believe whatever someone tells you about the law. Even websites that provide advice about the law are sometimes not entirely reliable. The information may be incomplete or out of date, or the people who wrote the information may have misinterpreted what the law says. In other words, if you want to get to know your legal rights and responsibilities, you need a trustworthy source of information.

Our goal is to provide you with such a source. Although we have tried to cover a lot of different topics, laws vary a lot from one part of the country to another, and we cannot cover all of them in one book. You may want to find out more about certain issues on your own. You can try to read the law yourself and see what it says, and we hope you will, but legal documents can be easier to make sense of if you know how to read them. We will tell you where to find some of the important laws and explain a little of how to understand them. We will also give references to some of the rules of the law in the book, so you can check what they say for yourself if you want, and we provide a glossary of legal terms in appendix A. Terms defined in the glossary appear in bold the first time we use them.

As we have said, the legal rights of children and teens in this country are currently rather limited, but laws have changed before, and they can change again. New laws are passed or existing ones altered when attitudes within a society change. Back in the nineteenth century, for instance, the law gave young people extremely few rights of their own. If a family needed money, children could be forced to work long hours in factories or in other jobs, rather than being given an education. Gradually, though, people came to feel that this was unfair, and so laws were passed that set limits on child labour. And, over the years, young people have continued to acquire greater rights. In 1970, for example, the voting age in Canada was lowered from 21 to 18, and now some people argue that it should be dropped further, to 16. Internationally, the United Nations has done much to challenge governments to respect the idea of "children's rights" or "youth rights." The United Nations Educational, Scientific and Cultural Organization (UNESCO) proclaimed 1979 to be the International Year of the Child, and, in 1989, the UN adopted the Convention on the Rights of the Child, about which we will have more to say in chapter 1. Canada **ratified** the Convention in 1991, and, today, numerous countries have laws that require adults to treat youth more like people whose opinions matter.

We find such changes encouraging, and we hope that you do as well. All the same, you will find that the rights youth have in this country, especially rights to make their own decisions, are very limited. We're disappointed that, despite recent improvements, the law still doesn't care very much about your need for independence. It's true that many laws are meant to protect you, perhaps because people suppose you to be immature and vulnerable. But these so-called protections often stop you from doing things just because you are under a fixed age, without giving you a chance to prove you might actually be capable of doing them. Getting a driver's licence is just one example of such things (see chapter 2). Not only does the law greatly limit even competent youth, but in our opinion it also doesn't require adults to pay nearly enough attention to young people's emotional needs. Perhaps, for instance, after reading chapter 3, you may come to believe as we do that the law should require judges to respect children's wishes when making decisions about parental **custody**.

These are just a few examples of the reasons why we think Canadian youth should be asking for more legal rights. At the same time, we will say very little in this book about exactly what rights we think you should have. That is a very complex question, and we encourage you to think for yourself about what rights adults should give you and to find good reasons why you should be given those rights.

There's a lot of information in this book, not only about specific laws but about your rights, about Canada's legal system, and about what you can (and cannot) expect to get from the law. We hope that this information will be useful to you—that it will answer questions you might have and show you how laws about young people affect your life. We also hope that you will think about the way the law treats youth and what it assumes about them. Finally, we hope that adults who read this book will stop to consider how our laws might do more to support and respect the basic human rights of children and youth in this country.

ACKNOWLEDGEMENTS

We wish to extend our heartfelt gratitude to Trish McCracken and E. Roy Harvey for providing information on how education law works in practice and to Police Sergeant (retd.) Jim Roberts for similar information about the enforcement of criminal and provincial laws. We would also like to thank everyone on the AU Press team, particularly our editor, Pamela Holway, for their relentless efforts in making this book a reality.

THE LAW IS

(NOT)

FOR KIDS

1

INTRODUCTION TO THE LAW AND YOUR RIGHTS

Before we start talking about specific laws, it would be useful if we explained where laws come from, what they look like, and where to find them. This information will give you a general sense of how the law operates. In addition, we would like to say something about the notion of rights and their relationship to the law, as well as about rights for children and youth.

One thing you should keep in mind from the start is that laws differ to some extent depending on where in Canada you live. Why is that? The answer has to do with how our country is set up. Canada is a **federation**: a country divided into smaller units—in our case, ten provinces and three territories—that have their own governments. In fact, Canada has *three* levels of government: the federal government, based in Ottawa; provincial and territorial governments; and local, or municipal, governments. Each of these levels of government has the power to make laws about certain things. For example, each province or territory gets to decide how old you have to be to get a driver's licence, while each city or town gets to decide where to build schools and hockey rinks. The part of the country in which a government's laws apply is called that government's **jurisdiction**. Laws made by the federal government apply to the entire country (except for a few that are meant to cover only some provinces or territories), whereas laws made by the two lower levels of government apply only in a particular province or territory or else only in a specific municipality. So precisely which sets of laws apply to you depends on where you live.

Many of the laws that affect young people are provincial laws, rather than federal ones. Your local government may also have laws that affect you—curfews, for instance. This means that the people who are responsible for enforcing these laws—such as police officers, social workers, public lawyers, or school principals—often work for either the province or territory in which you live or else for your local government. When you have a question or a problem, it's important to know which level of government deals with your issue and where you can go to find the help you need. This book will explain how to find these things out.

The powers of the federal government and of the provinces and territories to make laws are laid out in Canada's Constitution—specifically, in sections 91 and 92 of the Constitution Act, 1867.[1] If you need to prove your citizenship or if

1 Canada's Constitution (https://laws-lois.justice.gc.ca/eng/const/) has two main parts: the Constitution Act, 1867 and the Constitution Act, 1982. Appendix B provides an overview of our Constitution, and

you get married (see chapter 6), if you open a bank account (see chapter 2) or are convicted of a crime (see chapter 8), then you will encounter procedures and rules established by federal law. Citizenship, marriage, and divorce, the regulation of banking and commerce, and the establishment of federal penitentiaries are some of the many areas listed in section 91 of the 1867 Constitution Act in which the federal government is entitled to make laws. The federal government also has the power to define what counts as criminal behaviour.

However, if you want to make your own choices about which classes to take in school (see chapter 4), if you want to earn money with a part-time job (see chapter 5), or if your family is involved with social services (see chapter 7), then you are dealing with systems and rules that are under provincial or territorial jurisdiction. Section 92 of the 1867 Constitution Act grants provincial and territorial governments the power to make laws about many subjects, including employment and workers' rights, the education system, health and social services, and the ownership of property. In addition, provinces and territories hold jurisdiction in the area of *civil law* (also known as *private law*)—that is, rules that govern relations between private citizens, which include laws about how parents must treat children. Unlike federal laws, these laws apply only in a specific province or territory. As for the third level of

---

it also describes the basic structure of our government. You may already know how our government works—but if you don't, appendix B will help.

government, each province or territory is responsible for the municipalities that are found within it and can delegate certain powers to them. As a result, municipal governments—city councils, for example—can pass their own laws on local matters, such as zoning, street cleaning, recreational facilities, curfews, and garbage collection.

First Nations reserves are a special case. According to section 91 of the 1867 Constitution Act, the federal government has jurisdiction over "Indians, and Lands reserved for the Indians."[2] The relationship between the Canadian state and First Nations is laid out in detail in a document called the Indian Act (https://laws-lois.justice.gc.ca/eng/acts/i-5/), which was first written in 1876 and has since been amended several times (most recently in 2017), as well as in various treaties negotiated between specific bands—that is, First Nations groups—and the Canadian government. According to the Indian Act, reserve lands are held by the federal government: these lands do not belong to the province in which they are located. All the same, most provincial laws apply on reserves, and so do many federal laws, such as the Criminal Code of Canada. In addition, most reserves have their own governments, led by band councils or tribal councils, which are responsible for certain community matters such as policing, schools, and child welfare services. But the federal government still gives Indigenous communities only limited power to make their own decisions.

---

2 Today, the term "Indian" is used only in legal contexts. For the most part, the federal government gets to decide who is a "status Indian" (or a "registered Indian") and is thus eligible for certain benefits.

Enforcing the Law

When someone says "law enforcement," we usually think of the police arresting people who have committed a crime and should be punished for it. But laws are enforced not simply for the sake of punishing wrongdoers but in order to protect people's rights—and even someone who has broken the law has rights. After all, if no one enforced the law, there would be no point to having laws in the first place.

Government agencies employ many people who help to ensure that our rights under the law are respected and that we likewise respect the rights of others. Here are some of those who might be in a position to help you if you have a problem:

- The *police* are supposed to protect public safety, help people in danger, and enforce the law by arresting those who break it and taking them into **custody**. You will learn more about what they can and cannot do in chapter 8.

- *Social workers* are trained to help individuals, families, and communities cope with difficult situations. Some work in family service agencies, where they can help children and youth who are victims of abuse or neglect. Some work in other settings, like group homes and hospitals, where they can help individuals and families deal with other kinds of problems and challenges, such as health issues. You will find out more about what social workers do in chapter 7.

- *Ombudsmen* (sometimes called *ombudspersons* or simply *ombuds*) are public officials whose job is to help citizens who think that a public agency or office isn't respecting their rights. Most provinces and territories have an ombudsman for children, often called a child and youth advocate, who works to protect the rights of young people who must deal in some way with government agencies. Child and youth ombudsmen and advocates spend much of their time responding to the complaints of young people who are either in foster care or else involved with the criminal justice system, but they may also help youth who have other complaints. Appendix C provides a full list of youth advocates—and, in the last chapter in this book, you will find some ideas on how to advocate for yourself.

While all these people help to make sure that laws are obeyed, responsibility for enforcing the law ultimately lies with the judicial system—that is, judges and courts. The job of the courts is to resolve disputes and, beyond that, to oblige people to abide by the law and respect the rights of others. If someone is accused of a crime, it's up to the courts to determine whether enough evidence exists to find the person guilty and, if it does, then to decide what sort of punishment is appropriate. Although judges do have the power to send someone to jail, they can also order people simply to pay a fine and/or to do something to make up for what they have done wrong, such as honouring a contract or debt or performing a community service.

While going to court is one way to settle a dispute, not every dispute needs to end up in court. Less serious complaints can often be resolved by one of the many legal boards and tribunals that exist both at the federal level and in every province or territory. Most provinces and territories have a Labour Relations Board, for instance, while, at the federal level, examples include the Canada Industrial Relations Board, the Canadian Broadcast Standards Council, and the Canadian Human Rights Tribunal. These various boards and tribunals are not officially part of the court system, but they have the power to make judgments about specific questions or disputes that have a relatively limited scope and are therefore unlikely to have broader consequences or implications. If someone feels that the resulting judgment wasn't fair, there's always the option of taking the matter to court for further review.

Canada has several different kinds of courts, which are arranged in levels, from lower to higher:

- provincial or territorial courts (inferior courts)
- provincial or territorial superior courts
- provincial or territorial courts of appeal, the Federal Court of Appeal, and the Tax Court of Canada
- the Supreme Court of Canada

Provincial or territorial courts hear a wide range of civil cases (including those relating to youth), as well as some criminal cases. These cases can involve either federal laws or laws specific to that province or territory. Provincial or territorial superior courts hear especially serious criminal and civil cases and also serve as the first court of appeal in their area of jurisdiction. In several provinces, the superior court is called the Court of Queen's Bench, while several other provinces call their superior court the Supreme Court of that province.

Perhaps you have heard of someone **appealing** a judge's decision. This means they are asking a judge in a higher court to review the decision and decide whether it was fair. This is the task of the courts of appeal (also known as *appellate courts*) in each province and territory and likewise of the Federal Court of Appeal, which only considers cases that relate to federal laws. Some appeals go all the way up to the Supreme Court of Canada, the highest court in the land, which is the final place where decisions made by lower courts can be examined and reconsidered. The Supreme Court has nine judges—a chief justice and eight puisne (junior) justices—who work together to make the final decision.[3]

Judges are often asked to decide how a law should be interpreted and whether it applies in a particular case. In addition, the courts can rule on whether a law respects the Constitution. Both the Supreme Court and the superior courts in each province have the power to find a law

---

3 If you look at a Supreme Court decision, you'll see that the justices often write separate opinions, sometimes individually and sometimes jointly, in small groups. When one (or more) of the justices disagrees with the final decision, that justice writes a *dissenting* opinion. But even when all of the justices hearing a case agree on the final ruling, they may agree for different reasons, which is why they often write separate opinions—to explain their own reasoning.

unconstitutional. In that case, the law is invalid and can no longer be enforced.

So Where Do Laws Come From?

The law is a complex system, which is why we often need help from people like lawyers and ombudsmen, who understand how it works. The law is complicated partly because, as societies evolve, so does the law: new laws are passed, while others are revised or repealed. The Cannabis Act is a good example of this. Over the years, many Canadians had come to feel that marijuana was no more harmful than alcohol, and one of the things the Liberal party promised to do if elected in 2015 was to legalize cannabis.

But the law is also complicated because it comes from more than one place. We tend to think of "the law" as lists of rules neatly laid out in documents like the Criminal Code of Canada. But, while this is true of some laws, it's not true of the law as a whole. In most of Canada (Québec is the exception), there are two main kinds of law: **statutes** and **common law**. Statutes are laws that have been passed by Parliament or by provincial or territorial legislatures. A statute starts out as a **bill**, that is, a proposal to create new legislation or to alter an existing law. Once a bill is introduced into Parliament or a provincial or territorial legislature, it receives multiple rounds of discussion and debate before it is finally either passed into law or defeated (a process we describe in detail in appendix B). Statutory laws are collected in multi-volume publications such as the *Revised Statutes of Canada* or the *New Brunswick Acts and Regulations,* which makes them relatively easy to find.

In contrast, common law consists of a large body of rules that come from decisions made by the courts. These rules are not listed in one place but are found in the written decisions of judges in particular court cases (which is why common law is sometimes called "case law"). Today, there are thousands upon thousands of court decisions, so lawyers who are working on a case sometimes have to do a lot of research to find decisions that are relevant to their case. Common law started developing in England during the Middle Ages, when disputes were brought before the king's judges, who would then make decisions based on what seemed fair to them. Over time, as more and more cases were brought before courts, legal rulings piled up, and these rules collectively came to be known as common law.

The concept of a **precedent** is particularly important to common law. When a judge makes a decision in a new case (that is, a case unlike any of those that have previously come before the courts), the judge's decision in the case creates a *precedent*—a rule or a principle that judges are then expected to follow when deciding similar cases. The notion of following precedent is founded on a legal principle called *stare decisis,* which means "to stand by what was decided."

How far a judge is obliged to follow precedent depends on the level of the court. If the precedent was set in a lower court, then judges deciding similar cases at the same level of court are expected to regard this rule as *persuasive*. That is, they're supposed to take it into account and make decisions in a way that is consistent with the earlier decision. If the precedent was set in a higher court, however, judges in lower courts in that same province or territory *must* abide by this earlier rule when called upon to decide similar cases. In other words, a precedent established by a higher court is **binding** on lower courts in the same jurisdiction.[4] Similarly, if a legal ruling made by a higher court differs from an earlier ruling made by a lower court, then the new rule becomes the precedent, replacing the older one. However, unlike lower courts, higher courts are not bound by their own decisions. The Supreme Court, for example, may make a ruling and then, at some later date, when another case comes along, may decide to make a different ruling—in which case the newer rule again replaces the older one as the precedent.

If you look at some of the court cases listed in appendix D, you'll see that these decisions run to many pages. But not everything that a judge says in a written decision is part of the precedent—only the final decision itself and the parts of the judgment in which the judge explains the reasoning that led to the decision. In writing decisions, judges may make statements about how certain laws should be interpreted or how an existing law applies (or doesn't apply) in

---

4 The lower court judge may, however, argue that the facts of the earlier case were sufficiently different that the reasoning used by the higher court judge in reaching a decision can't really be applied to the case currently under consideration.

a particular situation. But unless these statements play an essential part in the judge's final decision, they are not binding—although other judges may draw on them for guidance in making decisions about future cases.[5]

This system means that, if you have a legal question, you won't necessarily find your answer in a statute: the answer may actually lie in a court decision, possibly one that was made decades ago. Having two different sources of law might seem like a recipe for confusion—so how do these two bodies of law work together? Simply put, statutes trump common law: a judge cannot make a decision that violates a statute. If, at some point, a new statute (or an amendment to an existing one) is enacted that differs from a rule of the common law, that rule is now invalid: judges must abide by the statute.

Finally, we should point out that the common law system is basically an English tradition. When it comes to matters of civil law, Québec doesn't rely on the system of common law used elsewhere in Canada. Instead, Québec law uses the Civil Code of Québec, a long list of rules and regulations that affect relations between private citizens (including family members) within the province. The use of a civil code is characteristic of French legal tradition.

---

5 In legal language, the parts of a decision that explain a judge's reasoning are called the *ratio decidendi*, "the reason for deciding." The term for incidental statements—statements that are not binding—is *obiter dicta*, that is, things that are "said in passing."

How Statutes Are Written

Statutes generally follow a standard written form, which always starts with a *title*. Normally, there will be a long version of the title and a short version, which is the commonplace name of the law. For example, "An Act in respect of criminal justice for young persons and to amend and repeal other Acts" is the long title of the statute whose short title is the "Youth Criminal Justice Act." Below the title, there may be a *preamble*—an opening section (usually fairly short) that explains the general purpose of the statute. For instance, the preamble of the Youth Criminal Justice Act contains the statement, "Canadian society should have a youth criminal justice system that commands respect, takes into account the interests of victims, fosters responsibility and ensures accountability through meaningful consequences and effective rehabilitation and reintegration, and that reserves its most serious intervention for the most serious crimes and reduces the over-reliance on incarceration for non-violent young persons." This sets out some of the general principles that the act is intended to serve.

Now let's look at how an actual statute is set up. If a statute is very long and detailed, its text may be divided into several *parts* or *divisions* to separate major topics. But, regardless of whether such part divisions exist, statutes are typically divided into numbered units called *sections*, which separate the text into specific points. Here is the beginning of section 29 of the Youth Criminal Justice Act (http://laws.justice.gc.ca/eng/acts/Y-1.5/index.html):

29. (1) A youth justice court judge or a justice shall not detain a young person in custody prior to being sentenced as a substitute for appropriate child protection, mental health or other social measures.

Justification for detention in custody

(2) A youth justice court judge or a justice may order that a young person be detained in custody only if

(a) the young person has been charged with

(i) a serious offence, or

(ii) an offence other than a serious offence, if they have a history that indicates a pattern of either outstanding charges or findings of guilt.

As you can see, section 29 is divided into smaller units, which are numbered in parentheses. These are called *subsections*. (Section 29 actually has a total of three subsections, but only the first one and part of the second are shown above.) "**Justification for detention in custody**" is a heading added for the convenience of readers to summarize the subject of subsection (2). Subsection (1) is not subdivided, but subsection (2) is further broken up into *paragraphs*, which are marked with lowercase letters in parentheses. This subsection is divided into paragraphs because there is more than one possible reason for a judge to decide to "order that a young person be detained in custody"—although we have shown you only the first possible reason, which is identified in paragraph (a). If you look at the act, you'll see that there are two more reasons, which are given in paragraphs (b) and (c). Paragraph (a) is then further divided into two *subparagraphs,* marked with lowercase roman numerals in parentheses: (i) and (ii). All statutes follow a similar system of organization, although the terms used for the different levels can vary a little. For example, many provincial statutes have *clauses* instead of paragraphs, while the Civil Code of Québec has *articles* instead of sections.

This kind of logical, methodical organization of a statute—breaking it down into sections, subsections, and so on—is very helpful for lawyers and judges. If a lawyer is arguing that a young person should not be kept in custody, the lawyer needs to give a good reason why, and that reason needs to be clearly justified by the law. So, for instance, the lawyer could point out that the young person in question has not been charged with "a serious offence" and then give the reason as "subparagraph 29(2)(a)(ii)" of the Youth Criminal Justice Act. This is where precedent can become important. Have there been other cases in which a closely similar offence was in fact judged to be serious—or explicitly judged *not* to be serious? The judge will need to consider those cases in order to decide whether the lawyer's argument is valid.

Legal language tends to be very precise. So, when you read a statute, you'll need to keep in mind the following points in order to understand exactly what it means:

- Statutory laws often use certain key terms in a very specific way. In such cases, the law will define these terms, usually in a separate section at the beginning of the law. These definitions apply only to that law; the same terms may have a slightly different meaning in another law. (Sometimes these definitions apply only to a specific part of the law, in which case they will appear at the beginning of that part.)

- When a statute says that someone *shall* do something, this means that the person has a duty to do it. In other words, you must do that thing. When a statute says that someone *may* do something, this means that the person has the option of doing it but is not obligated to do it. In our example here, the judge "may" detain in custody a young person who has been charged with a serious offence, but the judge doesn't have to do so.

- In legal language, if the word *and* appears before the last item in a list of conditions (a, b, *and* c), this means that *all* those conditions must be fulfilled in order for something to happen. If the word *or* is used instead of *and,* this means that only one of those conditions must be fulfilled. In our example here, the word *or* between subparagraphs 29(1)(a)(i) and 29(1)(a)(ii) means that the judge may detain the offender if the offence is "serious," even if there is no "history that indicates a pattern." Both conditions need not be present—one or the other is enough.

Existing statutes are constantly being amended. Rather than rewrite the whole law, an amendment to a statute will state what parts of the existing law are to be changed, either by indicating what part of the text is to be rewritten and how or else by adding new text. Sometimes it will be necessary to add whole sections between existing ones; this is usually done by using a decimal system. For example, when a new section about expulsion was added to Ontario's Education Act, this section logically fit between sections 311 and 312 of the existing act, so this new section was numbered 311.1.

Where to Find Laws

The common law, as we explained above, is found in a wide array of written court decisions, the text of which is published. In the case of statutes, the Department of Justice publishes full, up-to-date versions of important federal laws with all amendments in place on its Justice Laws Website (https://laws-lois.justice.gc.ca/eng/); these versions are the official ones. Provincial and territorial governments also publish their laws online. (Paper copies of statutes can be hard to get; they are mainly found in law and reference libraries.) However, the most comprehensive online resource is the website of the Canadian Legal Information Institute (CanLII): http://www.canlii.org/.

On its home page, the CanLII provides links to every major jurisdiction in Canada—federal and provincial or territorial. From there, you can access all the statutes and **regulations** (government orders that spell out specific legal procedures and requirements) currently in force in that jurisdiction. But you can also access decisions made by courts in each jurisdiction, as well as judgments made by boards and tribunals; these are organized by the name of the court or of the board or tribunal. For someone doing legal research, however, the greatest advantage to the site is its search function. It's not very difficult to figure out how to use the site, and it can be very useful.

Even so, trying to find the answer to a legal question all on your own can be challenging. For one thing, legal language tends to be very dull and dry (although this is partly because the wording of legal documents has to be very precise), and it can also be quite difficult to understand if you're not used to it. Moreover, once you've found a law that has to do with the topic you're researching and have located the part of the law that relates to your question, you may think you have the answer—but the full answer may actually be found in a combination of several laws or in several parts of one law or in a law plus one or more court decisions. It is particularly difficult to research court decisions, as cases can span many years and many courts—sometimes not only Canadian courts but British ones as well. For these reasons, if you have an actual legal problem of your own, it is best to talk to a lawyer or an ombudsman, who may already know what your rights are and what can be done in your situation. If not, they can certainly help you find out and make sure that the information you have is accurate and complete.

Laws and Rights

People often look to the law to protect their rights. But what exactly is a "right"? Basically, a right is a claim about what someone deserves or is owed. The right to free speech, for example, means that people deserve to be able to express their ideas and opinions. However, in order for a claim to be considered a right, the claim must be justified in some way. That is, the person claiming the right must be able to offer a convincing reason for why he or she is owed that thing. You could claim that you have a right not to do school homework, but you might have a hard time persuading your parents and teachers that this is indeed your right.

Pointing to an existing law is one way to justify the claim to a particular right. Rights that are backed up by laws are known as *legal* rights—although this isn't quite as simple as it sounds. Some laws actually do talk in terms of rights. For example, according to section 8 of Canada's Constitution Act, 1982, "Everyone has the right to be secure against unreasonable search or seizure." Often, though, the existence of a right is only implied in what a law says. To use our earlier example, paragraph 29(2)(a) of the Youth Criminal Justice Act says that a judge cannot keep a young person in custody unless that young person has either committed a serious offence or has a history of being arrested for less serious offences. From this, you can conclude that, as a young person, you have a legal right not to be kept in custody if neither of these conditions is present. But it can sometimes be hard to figure out, on the basis of what a law actually says, whether it upholds an underlying right (and, if so, what that right is). In fact, even when the law explicitly states that we have a right to be protected from an "unreasonable" search, there can be arguments about what sort of search is unreasonable.

To complicate matters further, not all rights are backed up by laws. Although the law gives us a means to justify our claim to a right, the ultimate justification for our most important rights is a shared sense of what is fair and what people naturally deserve to have or receive or be able to do. Such rights are sometimes called *moral* rights—rights that are justified on the basis of ethical principles that most human beings would probably defend. One very important example of such rights, which was created in 1948 by the United Nations, is the Universal Declaration of Human Rights (http://www.un.org/en/universal-declaration-human-rights/)—a list of thirty articles that describe the basic rights to which all human beings are entitled.

The only problem is that it can be difficult to enforce a moral right unless it is protected by law—and a declaration made by the United Nations doesn't have the binding force of a law. For example, article 5 of the Universal Declaration of Human Rights states: "No one shall be subjected to torture or to cruel, inhuman or degrading treatment or punishment." In Canada, this right is protected by section 12 of our 1982 Constitution Act, which reads: "Everyone has the right not to be subjected to any cruel and unusual treatment or punishment." Many other countries have similar laws, but not all do—and if they don't, then, despite the UN declaration, people in that country could legally be tortured. Furthermore, even when the law says you have a legal right to something, whether this right will actually be enforced can depend on how willing people in power are to protect your rights or on whether they have the resources they need to do so. This is one reason why we have ombudsmen and courts—so that we have a place to go if someone who is supposed to enforce our rights isn't doing so.

The most important statement about the rights of people who live in Canada is the Canadian Charter of Rights and Freedoms, which is part of the Constitution Act, 1982 (and from which the two examples above are drawn). The Charter contains a list of fundamental human, political, and civil rights that all levels of government and all laws made in Canada must respect. Many existing laws have been challenged in court because someone argued that they violated the Charter of Rights and Freedoms. In chapter 4, for instance, you will read about laws that have been changed because the courts have ruled that section 15 of the Charter, which, among other things, protects people from discrimination on the basis of "sex," also protects them against discrimination on the basis of sexual orientation.

In addition to the Charter of Rights and Freedoms, another federal law, called the Canadian Human Rights Act (https://laws-lois.justice.gc.ca/eng/acts/h-6/), also protects people against discrimination. This act, which was passed by Parliament in 1977, created the Canadian Human Rights Commission. In addition, provinces and territories have their own human rights legislation, such as the Ontario Human Rights Code, the Northwest Territories Human Rights Act, and Québec's *Charte des droits et libertés de la personne* (Charter of Human Rights and Freedoms). Like both the Canadian Charter of Rights and Freedoms and the Canadian Human Rights Act, provincial or territorial human rights acts generally prohibit discrimination on the basis of age. If you look closely, however, you'll see that a number of provinces explicitly define "age" to mean the age of majority and above. Moreover, most provincial or territorial acts contain specific rules relating to the age at which a person is eligible for something. In other words, when "discrimination" is prohibited, this is understood to mean *illegal* discrimination—and, when a question arises, it's up to the courts to decide what is illegal.

Do "Children's Rights" Exist?

At some point, you may have heard about the existence of "children's rights," "teen rights," or "youth rights." Such a list of rights does in fact exist; it's called the Convention on the Rights of the Child (http://www.ohchr.org/en/professionalinterest/pages/crc.aspx). This is an **international treaty**, which was formally adopted by the United Nations in 1989 and ratified by Canada in 1991, and it lays down rights that every young person in the world is entitled to have.

Although the earliest laws designed to protect children were passed back in the nineteenth century, the idea of children's rights is relatively new. In 1923, a British woman named Eglantyne Jebb, the founder of Save the Children, wrote what became the first international statement about children's rights, consisting of five brief points that summarized what children everywhere are entitled to. The following year, the League of Nations (the forerunner of the United Nations) adopted her statement, which came to be known as the Geneva Declaration of the Rights of the Child. In 1948, the UN General Assembly adopted a slightly expanded version (containing seven points), which became the basis for the UN's Declaration of the Rights of the Child, a set of ten principles adopted by the General Assembly in 1959. Like its predecessors, however, this was merely a declaration, which lacked the power to be legally binding. Then, in 1978, Poland proposed writing a Convention on the Rights of the Child. Unlike a declaration, a convention is an international treaty, which can be legally binding on the states that agree to it. So, in 1979, the UN set up a working group to write this convention. The group met in Geneva once a year, and it took them an entire decade to finish their work.

FACT FILE   **How Children Came to Have Rights**

For a very long time, no one really thought of children as having rights. We need not look far into our own history for evidence. Up to the early nineteenth century, the British government (which ruled over the entire British Empire) didn't much care how young people were treated, as long as they were not killed or maimed. Children were generally taught to respect and obey their parents and other adults and not to voice their own opinions, and many young people grew up with harsh physical punishments. Serious abuse often went unnoticed, for people tended to assume that the law should not meddle in the family. Young people from poor families tended to fare the worst. Many had to work under dangerous conditions, in factories and even mines, in order to help support themselves and their families. Some ended up living on the street, where they were reduced to begging or stealing. In addition, especially during the closing decades of the nineteenth century, poor children from Britain were transported to Canada (or elsewhere in the British Empire), where they were usually put to work, and in many cases their adoptive families treated them like slaves.

In Canada, Indigenous children were subjected to especially cruel treatment, in the form of residential schools. Beginning in the 1870s, Indigenous children were forcibly taken from their families and placed in these schools, where they were taught to be ashamed of their own language and culture—that is, of who they were. Under the threat of harsh punishment, they were expected to abandon their own customs and beliefs, convert to Christianity, and learn to respect Western values and standards of behaviour. Many of them were physically, sexually, and emotionally abused by the people who ran these schools. The devastating impact of this system is still felt today in Indigenous communities, although it took a long time for other people in Canada to recognize how much damage had been done. Finally, in 2008, a fact-finding group called the Truth and Reconciliation Commission began a lengthy investigation into what children experienced at residential schools. In December 2015, the TRC issued ninety-four "Calls to Action" (https://nctr.ca/assets/reports/Calls_to_Action_English2.pdf), which include recommendations designed to improve the health and welfare of Indigenous children. But there is still a great deal of work to be done in this area.

Non-Indigenous children were more fortunate. During the late nineteenth century, social reformers in both Britain and North America steadily fought to improve the conditions under which many young people lived, especially in crowded urban areas. In 1891, a branch of the Children's Aid Society opened in Toronto, and two years later, Ontario passed the first provincial law prohibiting cruelty to children. Similar legislation soon followed elsewhere in Canada. These early laws focused mainly on preventing harsh and exploitative treatment and limiting child labour, as well as on providing compulsory public education. That is, the emphasis fell on *protecting* children who had been abandoned or victimized by adults.

During the early decades of the twentieth century, social consciousness began to shift. Workers struggled for better wages and working conditions, women argued for the right to vote, and, in many of Britain's colonies, subjugated peoples began fighting for independence. In addition, many people were appalled by the slaughter that took place during the First World War, and humanitarian ideals began to take root. As people became more aware of the impact of trauma and learned to be more sensitive to children's emotional needs, they began to see young people as developing human beings who have rights like anyone else.

The Convention on the Rights of the Child was adopted by the UN General Assembly on November 20, 1989. Since then, it has been ratified by all the countries in the world except for the United States (which has signed it but has never ratified it). No other international treaty has achieved virtually universal acceptance. So what does this Convention say?

What the Convention on the Rights of the Child Says

The Convention is made up of a preamble and fifty-four articles, divided into three parts. Among other things, the preamble affirms that the rights and freedoms listed in the Universal Declaration of Human Rights apply to all people (including children), that it is necessary to give particular care to children and the family, and that children should be fully prepared to live an individual life in society. The first article then defines a "child" as any human being under the age of 18, except in places where, according to law, majority (legal adulthood) is attained at an earlier age.

The rights of children are laid out in the first part of the Convention (articles 1 to 41). Although the Convention itself does not divide these rights into categories, they are often viewed as falling into one of four groups: rights relating to survival, development, protection, and participation.

Survival rights entitle you to those things that keep you alive, safe, and in good health. They include:

- The right to expect your survival and development to be ensured to the maximum extent possible (article 6)

- The right to a name and nationality (article 7)

- The right to the highest possible standard of health (article 24)

- The right to a standard of living adequate for your development (article 27)

Development rights are meant to help you grow in a healthy, well-balanced way and learn what you need to be a responsible adult. They include:

- The right to know and be cared for by your parents (article 7)

- The right not to be separated from your parents without a good reason (article 9)

- The right to an education that develops your potential and values (articles 28 and 29)

- The right to opportunities for rest, play, and recreation (article 31)

Protection rights are meant to keep you safe from things that could harm your physical, mental, and emotional well-being. These rights include:

- Protection from unlawful interference with your privacy, family, and correspondence (article 16)

- Protection from all forms of violence, physical, emotional or sexual abuse, neglect, and exploitation (article 19)

- The right of disabled children to special care necessary to promote their development (article 23)

- The right to certain protections in armed conflicts (article 38)

Participation rights are meant to give you a say in matters that affect you and also confirm that various civil rights that adults have apply to young people as well. They include:

- The right to be free from discrimination on the basis of your or your parents' race, skin colour, sex, language, religion, political beliefs, national, ethnic, or social origin, disability, or other status (article 2)

- The right to freely express your opinion on matters affecting you and to have your opinion taken into account in a manner consistent with your maturity (article 12)

- The right to freedom of expression, as well as the right to search for, receive, and share information through different media (article 13)

- The right to freedom of thought, conscience, and religion (article 14)

In short, the Convention suggests that young people deserve to be given more rights than they often are. Yet one important question that the Convention *does not* clearly answer is, to what extent are young people entitled to make their own decisions and exercise their rights *independently*? Not one article explicitly mentions the right to certain freedoms from adult control. This silence reflects the way in which the Convention was written. The working group was very large, and it operated on the principle of consensus: it had to arrive at a wording on which everyone could agree. But different cultures have different views on when and in what circumstances children are entitled to some degree of independence. Some members of the group favoured giving young people more freedom to make their own decisions, without needing permission from adults, while others felt that adults have a duty to place limits on children's freedom in order to protect them. So, in the end, the solution was to leave the question open.

To take one example, according to article 5, States Parties (that is, states that are party to the Convention) agree to respect the "responsibilities, rights and duties" of parents and other guardians "to provide, in a manner consistent with the evolving capacities of the child, appropriate direction and guidance in the exercise by the child of the rights recognized in the present Convention." This means that parents are supposed to take a child's level of maturity into account when deciding how much direction and guidance to provide. What the article doesn't say is how long parents and other guardians can go on making decisions for a child that go against the child's own wishes. Similarly, article 14 states that, while children have the right to freedom of thought, conscience, and religion, States Parties must respect the right of parents to direct the child in the exercise of this right "in a manner consistent with the evolving capacities of the child." Does that mean that parents can force their child to practice a religion even when the child objects—and, if so, until when can they do this? The Convention doesn't say.

Yet even if the Convention doesn't explicitly give you the right to make your own decisions whenever you feel ready to do so, it does give you a lot of important rights that adults are supposed to respect. But do they have a legal obligation to do so? In Canada, the answer is no.

The Convention Is Not Law Everywhere

Although, as an international treaty, the Convention has the potential to be legally binding, ratifying the Convention does not automatically mean that it becomes part of that country's law. In fact, the power of the Convention is limited in two important ways. First of all, many of the countries that ratified it did so with "reservations." In other words, they indicated that they may not respect one or more of its articles or that they intend to accept only part of what an article says. While this option makes it more likely that countries will ratify the Convention, it also has the potential to weaken the power of the Convention.[6] Second, individual countries have the right to decide whether the Convention will be legally binding. In some countries, international conventions, once ratified, must be obeyed, just like the country's own laws. But in Canada, although lawmakers are supposed to *respect* such treaties, they are not legally bound to do so. This is why section 43 of the Criminal Code, which allows children to be physically punished, remains in force, even though section 19 of the Convention obliges States Parties to take appropriate measures—including legislative ones—to protect children from "all forms of physical or mental violence." (As we will see in chapter 3, the Supreme Court has at least placed certain limits on section 43.)

In short, the Convention on the Rights of the Child *is not a law in Canada but more of a moral agreement*. No one, not even the government, can be legally forced to abide by any of its rules.

But this doesn't mean that the Convention has no influence in Canada. For one thing, the United Nations has a Committee on the Rights of the Child, which monitors how

---

6 This is not to say that the *all* reservations expressed seriously undermined the Convention. For example, Canada has expressed two reservations. First, we may choose not to respect article 21, which concerns adoption, to the extent that this article is inconsistent with customary forms of care among Indigenous peoples. Second, Canada reserves the right to ignore article 37(c), which says that children "deprived of liberty" (that is, held in custody) should be detained separately from adults, when it is not appropriate or feasible to do so. In expressing these reservations, we were not trying to deny children their rights under the Convention but rather to ensure that these rights don't trample on other rights.

well countries are complying with the Convention. Every five years, all States Parties, including Canada, send a report to the committee, in which they describe what they have done to ensure that the Convention is respected. If nothing else, this puts pressure on Canada to bring forward legislation that would give some of the rights laid out in the Convention the force of law. Moreover, in drafting new laws (or amending existing ones) and in making court decisions, our lawmakers and judges do try to take the Convention into account, even if they aren't legally obligated to do so. Perhaps, in one way, it isn't such a bad thing that the Convention isn't law in Canada. As we have seen, some of the articles in the Convention appear to give parents and guardians some powers to decide when to limit a young person's independence. If *everything* in the Convention were legally binding in Canada, this might actually make it more complicated to pass new laws that could give young people greater freedom to make their own decisions, as these laws would conflict with parts of the Convention.

All in all, then, what the laws of Canada say about children and youth has a much greater impact on your rights than does the Convention on the Rights of the Child. Existing laws are also your best protection in cases of neglect, abuse, or exploitation. However, knowing about the Convention gives you a useful place to start should you wish to advocate for greater rights and freedoms. For example, if you think they will listen, you can talk to the adults in your life about the Convention and the rights it recommends that young people be given. Many of them may not realize that

Canada has agreed, at least in principle, to respect the rules in the Convention. Moreover, as you read through this book, you can compare the laws that currently govern your life to what the Convention says about the rights of children and young people. How well the law of the land actually respects these rights is a question well worth asking.

BEING A MINOR

The **age of majority** is the point at which, in the eyes of the law, a "child" becomes an "adult." Until you reach that age, the law considers you to be a **minor**, and many restrictions are placed on your rights and freedoms. For many years, Canadian law—like the law in many other places—regarded you as a minor until you reached the age of 21. During the second half of the twentieth century, however, many countries in the world, including Canada, lowered that age, usually to 18. But this doesn't mean that all 18-year-olds in Canada are legal adults. In fact, the age of majority is set not by the federal government but the laws of each province or territory. According to these laws, you reach the age of majority at 18 in six provinces: Alberta, Manitoba, Ontario, Prince Edward Island, Québec, and Saskatchewan. Elsewhere—that is, in British Columbia, New Brunswick, Newfoundland and Labrador, the Northwest Territories, Nova Scotia, Nunavut, and the Yukon—you need to wait until you turn 19.

Being a minor (or, as the law sometimes puts it, being an "infant," a "child," or someone "underage") mainly means the following things:

- You have a guardian or guardians—usually, but not always, your parents—who have certain powers over you and responsibilities toward you.

- You have only limited **legal capacity**. In other words, the number of legal acts that you are allowed to perform in your own name is quite small. For example, there are limitations on your ability to sell property and to sign a legally binding contract.

- You are generally held less responsible than an adult for contracts (promises you have made), for damages (compensation that a court decides you owe someone as a result of something you did wrong), and for criminal offences (until you're 18).

While many restrictions on your legal rights are tied to the age of majority, not all are. As we are about to see, you are legally allowed to do some things at a younger age. Some of these age restrictions pertain to broad areas, such as inheriting property or consenting to medical treatment, but let's begin by looking at how the law treats minors with regard to some commonplace issues.

Age Restrictions in Day-to-Day Life

Most of the age restrictions that you encounter as a minor will probably involve relatively commonplace situations—although this doesn't mean that these situations aren't important. In fact, they *are* important simply because they affect your everyday life. So here are some of the areas in which age restrictions typically apply.

> Alcohol, Tobacco and E-Cigarettes, and Narcotics

The age at which you may buy alcohol is 19 in all provinces and territories except for Alberta, Manitoba, and Québec, where the age is 18. Other laws place restrictions on who may provide you with alcohol, but these restrictions vary from province to province. For example, your parents may give you alcohol at home or in a private place at any age, in all provinces and territories except Nova Scotia and Newfoundland and Labrador.

The age at which you may buy tobacco is 18 in Alberta, Manitoba, the Northwest Territories, Québec, Saskatchewan, and the Yukon. It is 19 in British Columbia, New Brunswick, Newfoundland and Labrador, Nova Scotia, Nunavut, Ontario, and Prince Edward Island. The federal Tobacco and Vaping Products Act prohibits the sale of e-cigarettes to persons under 18, but, in many provinces, you must be 19 in order to purchase or use vaping products. As a general rule, vaping is prohibited in places where smoking is likewise banned.

Most provinces and the Yukon now ban smoking inside a car when a young person is present. You have the right to protection from second-hand smoke in a car until you are 16 in British Columbia, Manitoba, New Brunswick, Newfoundland and Labrador, Ontario, Québec, and Saskatchewan;

until you are 18 in the Yukon; and until you are 19 in Nova Scotia and Prince Edward Island. In most provinces, these regulations now extend to vaping in cars.

People who sell you alcohol or tobacco while you are underage are breaking the law, and you should expect them to ask you to show proper identification (ID) to prove your age. Depending on the province you are in, you can be punished if you are caught using false ID or possessing or consuming alcohol underage.

Possessing and selling most recreational drugs (these include cocaine, heroin, and crystal meth) is illegal for *anyone* of any age according to the federal Controlled Drugs and Substances Act. Cannabis, or marijuana, is no longer illegal for *everyone*, but it is still a controlled substance. Federal law allows people with certain health problems to purchase medical marijuana from licensed sellers, and now the Cannabis Act allows adults to possess small amounts of cannabis when in a public place (up to 30 grams of dried cannabis or the equivalent), to buy it from a licensed seller, and to grow up to four plants at home. These limits are important for you to know. There are other important restrictions spelled out in the Cannabis Act as well, which apply to young people in particular. For one thing, the law *strictly forbids providing marijuana to anyone under 18,* and adults who break this law face up to fourteen years in jail (ss. 9[1] and 9[5]). This new law also forbids young people (defined here as youth aged 12 to 17) to possess or distribute more than 5 grams of dried cannabis or the equivalent (ss. 8[1] and 9[1]); offenders face a youth sentence under the Youth Criminal Justice Act (ss. 8[2] and 9[5]). Furthermore, provincial and municipal governments may set stricter rules for selling cannabis and also lay down a higher minimum age than the federal one. Currently, the minimum age is 19 in all provinces and territories except for Alberta and Québec, which have retained the federal minimum age of 18.[1]

> Bank Accounts

Although the law does not restrict your right to open a bank account, banks themselves usually choose to limit minors' abilities to do so. Typically, for a child or youth to open an account, a bank will require the permission of a parent or guardian. The bank might also give your parent or guardian the option of controlling whether you can have a debit card or even whether you can withdraw money from your own account. One exception is the Royal Bank of Canada, which allows you to open a "Leo's Young Savers Account" or other youth account without a parent or guardian's signature if you are at least 13 years old and can show them proof of address and one piece of government-issued photo ID or two pieces of other valid ID, such as your birth certificate and your SIN (social insurance number) card.

---

1 Links to official information for the various jurisdictions can be found on the federal government's "Cannabis in the Provinces and Territories" page, https://www.canada.ca/en/health-canada/services/drugs-medication/cannabis/laws-regulations/provinces-territories.html.

> Curfews

Curfew laws that target young people are relatively common in the United States, but Canada is by no means free from them.[2] Ontario even has a provincial curfew. According to section 136(4) of the Child, Youth and Family Services Act, 2017, no parent may allow a child who is under 16 to loiter in a public place or to be in a place of public entertainment between midnight and 6 a.m. unless the parent either accompanies the child or allows someone 18 or older to do so.[3] Subsection (5) adds that if someone who is under 16 (or who appears to be under 16) is in a public place between midnight and 6 a.m. without an accompanying parent or adult (someone over 18), the police can apprehend the young person, who will either be taken home to his or her parents or, if that's not possible, then brought to some other safe place. Furthermore, the parents can be fined up to $5,000 and/or imprisoned for up to one year (s. 142[1]), although the police may choose only to issue them a warning.

In some towns, if a youth violates a curfew, only his or her parents can be punished, but, in others, the youth can also be fined—a rare example of a **status offence**

2 On curfews in the US, see, for instance, Tony Favro, "Youth Curfews Popular with American Cities but Effectiveness and Legality Are Questioned," *USA Today*, July 21, 2009, http://www.citymayors.com/society/usa-youth-curfews.html.

3 To "loiter" means to hang out somewhere for no apparent purpose. For example, sitting on a park bench after midnight may be considered loitering, but walking home after midnight shouldn't be. Theoretically, the police shouldn't apprehend you if you're walking home late, even if you look like you're under 16.

(something that is illegal only because a person is under-age), most of which no longer exist in Canada. The extent to which all these rules are actually enforced varies from place to place; in practice, youth are often given a warning and fines are rare.

Many have argued that curfew laws violate the Charter of Rights and Freedoms, specifically section 7, which grants the right not to be deprived of liberty and security of the person, and section 15, which grants equality under the law regardless of—among other things—age. In some communities, curfews have actually been revoked out of a concern that such laws may in fact be unconstitutional. A good case could probably be made in court on this matter. Curfews are mainly intended to reduce youth crime, but there is little strong evidence that they actually do so to any great extent, and they punish youth who would do nothing harmful at night in public. Still, some curfew laws are still in place, so you might want to find out what the law in your community says, just in case.

> Driver's Licences

The minimum age and conditions for getting a driver's licence vary somewhat from one province or territory to another and also depend on the kind of vehicle you want to drive. For driving a car, you typically have to be 16 to apply for your first licence. Generally, all new drivers are expected to start on a learner's permit, so a 16-year-old will usually have to pass a written test in order to get a learner's permit and then will have to pass a certain period, often twelve months, during which he or she will be allowed to drive only with an experienced driver in the passenger seat, before taking the road test for the next level of licence. But sometimes you can get a permit to drive another kind of vehicle at a younger age. (In New Brunswick, for example, you can apply for a motor-driven cycle licence or a tractor licence at the age of 14.) In the three territories, the minimum age to apply for a learner's permit is 15, and the minimum age to take the road test for a licence to drive without accompaniment is 16. In Alberta, when you are 14 you can actually get a "Class 7 licence"—a learner's permit—which allows you to drive a two-axle car accompanied by a licensed driver aged 18 or older; but you have to wait until you are 16 before you are allowed to take the road test for a "Class 5 licence," which allows you to drive alone. For other vehicles in Alberta, you need to be either 16 (to drive a motorcycle) or 18 (to drive a taxi, ambulance, or bus). Parental permission is also necessary in a number of provinces or territories. In Alberta, for instance, until you are 18, you must have your parents' permission in order to get a driver's licence, unless you are married or are supporting yourself.

Sometimes, special restrictions may apply to young drivers. In Ontario, for example, even after you earn your G2 licence (the first licence that allows you to drive without an experienced driver in the passenger seat), if you are 19 or younger and driving at night (between midnight and 5 a.m.), you may not normally carry more than one passenger who is also aged 19 or younger during the first six months of having your G2 licence. And, during the next six months, you may not carry more than three passengers of that age between midnight and 5 a.m., unless you turn 20 within that time.

> Gun Licences

If you are under 18, you may not "acquire" (buy or be given as your own property) a firearm or a crossbow (Firearms Act, s. 8[4]), nor may you import one into Canada. There are two possibilities for you to legally use someone else's gun: with a minor's licence or under the close supervision of an adult who has a licence for the gun you are using. You can apply for a minor's licence by going to the Chief Firearms Officer (an official of the RCMP) nearest to you.[4] Their office may issue the licence to you when you turn 12, allowing you to use a gun for hunting, target practice, in an organized shooting competition, or when being taught how to use it (s. 8[3]). You may get a licence even before the age of 12 if you need to be able to hunt or trap to help support yourself or your family (s. 8[2]). Your minor's licence will expire when you turn 18 or on its expiry date, whichever comes first; then you will have to apply for a regular licence before you can continue to use firearms.

A minor's licence carries quite a few restrictions: a parent or guardian must agree (s. 8[5]), and the Chief Firearms Officer may place conditions on when and how you may use the gun. You must complete the Canadian Firearms Safety

---

4 The RCMP provides contact information for the Chief Firearms Officer in each province and territory at http://www.rcmp-grc.gc.ca/cfp-pcaf/cfo-caf/index-eng.htm ("Chief Firearms Officers").

Course and pass a test (s. 7[1][a]), unless you need to hunt or trap to support yourself or your family (s. 7[4][b]). The licence allows you to use a normal rifle or shotgun but not a weapon that the law classifies as "prohibited" or "restricted" (s. 8[4]), such as a pistol or machine gun. You may also use your licence to buy ammunition, although some provinces or territories may place restrictions on your right to do so. If you don't have a minor's licence, you may borrow and use any kind of firearm if the owner has a licence for that class of gun, as long as he or she carefully supervises you while you use it, and as long as you only use it in the manner in which the owner may lawfully use it (para. 33[b]).

> Lotteries and Gambling

Such activities as placing bets on horse races, gambling in a casino, or playing the lottery are generally restricted to adults. You need to be 18 to buy a lottery ticket in Alberta, Manitoba, the Northwest Territories, Nunavut, Ontario, Québec, Saskatchewan, and the Yukon, and 19 in British Columbia, New Brunswick, Nova Scotia, Newfoundland and Labrador, and Prince Edward Island. Raffles tend to fall under similar age restrictions. In some provinces, you may be allowed to purchase a ticket, but if you win, the prize may have to be delivered to your parents or guardians. Or a government official may keep it for you until you reach the age of majority.

You may not gamble in a casino until the age of 19 in most of Canada, or until the age of 18 in Alberta, Manitoba and Québec. These age restrictions are generally the same for other games of chance, such as betting on horse races, betting on sports teams, or playing in a bingo hall.

> Movies and Video/DVD Rental

All provinces and territories except for Newfoundland and Labrador have rules about ratings for movies that theatres (and in some provinces, those who sell or rent videos or DVDs) must follow before they admit you. Even in New-foundland and Labrador, where movies are not rated, a theatre may refuse to admit you to a movie it considers inappropriate for your age. Each movie is rated by a board that decides how appropriate it is for people of different ages; some provinces have their own ratings boards, while some provinces use other provinces' ratings. Most provinces use, to a greater or lesser extent, a scheme similar to the Canadian Home Video Rating System, which classifies movies as follows:

G General audiences: anyone can see the movie.

PG Parental guidance: the theatre may admit anyone, but parents are advised that some things in the movie may not be suitable for all children.

14A People younger than 14 should be accompanied by an adult.

18A People younger than 18 should be accompanied by an adult.

R Restricted: only people 18 or over may see the movie (typically, a film containing pornography or graphic violence, brutality or other disturbing content).

E   Exempt: contains material not subject to classification (such as documentaries, music, or educational films).

> Names

When you are born, the name you get is largely left to the judgment of your parents. There are few rules limiting their choice, and if parents wish to give a child a name that is bizarre or somehow impractical, they can usually do so. However, it might rarely happen that the provincial registrar's office challenges or even refuses to register a name it considers to be particularly inappropriate. In extreme cases, a court may have to make the final decision. For example, in Québec (see article 54 of the Civil Code), if the parents can't be persuaded to reconsider their choice, the registrar can notify the Attorney General, who can then choose to bring the matter before a court.

In order to change your name without your parents' permission, you normally have to be over the age of majority—although, for example, New Brunswick allows 16-year-olds to apply for a name change on their own. Your parents can also apply to have your name changed. This sometimes happens following a divorce, when the parent who has custody of the children remarries and wants the entire family to have the step-parent's last name. Depending on the province, there may be an age from which your parents cannot normally change your name without your permission. In Alberta, British Columbia, and Ontario, for instance, that age is 12, whereas, in Québec, it's 14.

> Passports and Travel Outside of Canada

If you are under 16, a parent or legal guardian must apply for a passport for you. If you are 16 or over, you can apply on your own as an adult. When applying for a passport in Canada, you have to show certain documents that prove your identity and must have someone who can confirm that you are who you say you are agree that you may list them on the application form. You then give or send the application to a Passport Office or a Service Canada Passport Receiving Agent location, along with a fee.[5]

As a general rule, minors are not allowed to cross the Canadian border without the permission of their parents. If a young person from another country comes into Canada either unaccompanied or not accompanied by both of his or her parents, the border authorities will want to see a letter of authorization from the parent(s) not travelling with the minor, along with a photocopy of that parent's identification or passport.[6] A Canadian youth travelling to another country would probably be subject to similar rules there.

---

5 For instructions and forms, see "How to Apply for a New Passport," https://www.canada.ca/en/immigration-refugees-citizenship/services/canadian-passports/new-adult-passport/apply.html.

6 For more information, see "Minor Children Travelling to Canada," https://www.canada.ca/en/immigration-refugees-citizenship/services/visit-canada/minor-children-travelling-canada.html.

Sometimes, when parents have serious conflicts between them, one of them will try to abduct a child and take him or her to another country. This might be done by a parent who does not get custody of a child after divorce and who wants to take the child somewhere where that parent will be able to have the child to himself or herself, or it may be done by a parent who wants to stop the other parent from being able to make decisions for the child. Often, he or she can be stopped from doing so by police and border authorities if they are alerted on time about the abduction.

> Tattoos and Body Piercing

Laws on this can vary. In Newfoundland and Labrador, for instance, until you are 16, a shop can offer to tattoo you or give you body piercings only with your parents' consent, and you cannot be served in a tanning parlour or offered certain extreme body modification services (such as tongue bifurcation) until you are 19. Some other provinces (such as Alberta) have no laws on tattooing, but many shops will have policies that they will not provide these services until you are a certain age, at least not without parental consent.

> Voting

In Canada, the voting age and the age of majority are set by separate laws. Everyone can vote at the age of 18, even if the age of majority in their province or territory is 19. This is true not only for federal elections (according to section 3 of the Canada Elections Act) but also for provincial or territorial elections and municipal elections (as specified in the laws of each province and territory), as well as for band council elections, unless the First Nation has its own rules. In addition, 18 is the age at which you may be a candidate in a federal, provincial, territorial, or municipal election.

The voting age of 18 makes Canada typical, as this is the age at which you can vote in most countries around the world. A few countries, such as Austria, Brazil, and Scotland (for elections to the Scottish Parliament and for local elections), have lowered the voting age to 16, which is probably the lowest in the world. In other places, the voting age is higher than 18, such as Samoa, where it is 21.

> Other Age Restrictions

There are various other areas in which age restrictions may or do apply. Here are a few of them that may be useful to know about:

- You may apply to join the Canadian Forces at the age of 16 for the reserves and at the age of 17 for the regular force. Until you are 18, however, you need the written permission of at least one of your parents or guardians to join up (National Defence Act, s. 20[3]), and you cannot be sent to fight in a war or other hostilities (s. 34).

- According to federal law, the age at which you can get a pilot's licence varies depending on the type of licence. You can get a Student Pilot Permit at the age of 14 and a Recreational Pilot Permit at 16. But you must be 17 to get a Private Pilot License, 18 to get a

Commercial Pilot License (which allows you to fly only a single-pilot plane), and 21 to get an Airline Transport Pilot Licence—the professional licence that allows you to be the pilot in command of an aircraft that has a crew.

- Most provinces have laws requiring that minors wear bicycle helmets. In some places, these laws apply to adults as well.

As a minor, you may encounter other age restrictions, although we hope we've covered the most common ones. However, in addition to these relatively specific rules, there are a number of broad areas in which the law limits the legal capacity of minors, which are described below. Even if you never have to deal with some of these situations, they reveal a lot about the attitude of the law toward young people.

Contracts

Contracts are agreements between two (or occasionally more) people or groups of people in which each side promises to do something in exchange for something the other side promises to do. A contract spells out rights and responsibilities on both sides. If you get your own mobile phone, for example, you will sign a contract with your service provider. Similarly, if you rent an apartment, you will sign a contract—generally called a lease or a rental agreement—with your landlord. By signing a lease, you promise to give the landlord a sum of money, paid in full and on time, for the use of an apartment that belongs to your landlord—who, in turn, promises to make repairs to the property when needed and otherwise maintain it in decent shape. Contracts are legal obligations that can be enforced in court. In fact, an entire branch of the law—called, not surprisingly, *contract law*—deals with contractual agreements and with violations of them.

A contract is often a written agreement, which becomes valid—and hence enforceable in court—when both parties sign it. However, not every contract needs to be written out in order to be valid. Every time you buy something in a store, for example, you enter into an unwritten contract with the store: you agree to give the store money in exchange for the goods that the store gives you. If you fail in your legal duty to provide the money, the store does not have to give you the goods. But the contract also obliges the store to provide the goods in the state you expect them to be in (for example, they must not be broken). If the store doesn't do so, then you have a legal right to a refund or to better goods. Such a contract is valid even though no paper was signed.

According to Canadian common law, minors may generally enter into contracts of their own free will, without requiring permission from an adult. However, in some circumstances, these contracts may not be considered valid. First, a court may **void** (cancel) a contract if it finds that a young person was not mature enough to enter into the contract. For example, a 10-year-old may be considered mature enough to purchase a bicycle but not to sign a contract for a mobile phone. Second, the court may void a contract if it finds that the contract is not in a minor's best interests or that the other party is attempting to take advantage of a young person. If someone sells you something that isn't worth the price you agree to pay for it, the court may decide that you have been taken advantage of and void the contract.

Moreover, since the law regards minors as not yet fully mature, it actually allows you to **repudiate** most contracts within a reasonable period of time—in other words, to refuse to fulfill your part of the bargain. For instance, if you bought a new phone and then decided you didn't want it, you could reject the contract a day or two later and cancel the deal. As long as you returned the phone, the shop that sold it to you could not make you pay for it—whereas, if you were an adult, the shop could simply refuse to take the phone back (and could even take you to court if you refused to make good on the payment).

There is one exception to this rule, however: the law does not allow you to back out of an agreement (such as a lease) into which you have entered in order to procure the "necessaries of life"—that is, basic necessities such as enough food to eat, adequate clothing, and a place to live. In addition, provinces may have laws that extend a minor's legal obligation to honour a contract to other situations. In British Columbia, for instance, according to section 19.1(2) of the Infants Act, if a minor enters into a student loan agreement, that agreement is as binding on him or her as it would be for an adult.

As we explained in the previous chapter, Québec does not follow the common law tradition. With regard to minors and contracts, however, the law in Québec is basically very similar to the law elsewhere in Canada. As a general rule, when it comes to legal matters, minors in Québec must be represented by their "tutor" (the term used in Québec law for a child's parents or other guardians) — *except* in matters in which the law allows minors to act alone, as if they were adults (Civil Code, article 158). With respect to contracts, the Civil Code identifies two broad areas in which minors may act independently. First, as a minor, you may enter into contracts alone in order to meet your "ordinary and usual needs," as long as you are old enough and have sufficient "power of discernment" (that is, good enough judgment) to do so (article 157). Second, once you reach the age of 14, you are considered to be an adult in matters relating to your employment or your practice of a craft or profession (article 156), and so you can also enter alone into contracts in these areas. Otherwise, you would need to have your parents (or other guardians) enter into a contract on your behalf, which means that the contract would need to meet with their approval (especially since they would be liable for the consequences).

The fact that the law regards minors as too young to necessarily know what they're doing when they sign a contract is something of a mixed blessing. Yes, under common law, you can refuse to honour a contract — you can back out of the deal — and in most cases you will not be held liable, which means that you cannot be forced to make good on your promise. However, precisely because you are not held responsible for many contracts, many people will refuse to conclude them with you as long as you are a minor. We have already explained that many banks will not let you open your own bank account. Some landlords may refuse to rent you an apartment until you turn 18—although this is one situation in which the law may give you some protection because renting a place to live involves a necessity of life, namely, shelter. In Ontario, for instance, according to section 4 of the Ontario Human Rights Code, if you are 16 or 17 and have withdrawn from parental control (something we'll get into in the next chapter), a landlord may not discriminate against you because of your age. Such laws also mean, however, that once you've signed the rental contract, you can't repudiate it either.

Owning Property and Making Wills

As long as you're a minor, your rights to manage your own property, especially real estate (land and the buildings on it) and other items of high value, are severely restricted. Generally, if you inherit property from someone who has died, or if you buy or are given real estate, you cannot take control of that property yourself. So, for example, if your grandparents left you a valuable painting, you would not be able to sell it while you are still a minor. Instead, a guardian will manage your property for you until you come of age. In some places, including Québec (see article 192 of the Civil Code), your parents can perform this role, but often your guardian will be someone else, such as a government official called a *public guardian* or a *public trustee* (depending on where you are). Similarly, Québec's Civil Code (article 210) allows someone to leave you property on the condition that it be managed by a person other than your parents.

In some provinces, real estate can be registered in your name, even if an adult has to manage it for you; in others, public records will list that real estate under your guardian's name until you become an adult and can take possession in your own name. A guardian's exact powers vary from province to province, but they can include using income from your property to pay for the cost of maintaining it. Your guardian may even be able to sell your property if he or she thinks that this would be in your best interests, although doing so might require a court's permission. Once you reach the age of majority, a guardian must generally hand your property over to you and may also have to provide you with an account of how he or she has managed that property for you.

Under Québec law, you are allowed to control money that you have earned from work or that has been given to you in the form of allowances for your everyday needs. If these revenues become "considerable," however, your parents or guardians can ask a court to fix the amount that remains under your management. In determining this amount, the court will consider a number of factors, including your age and your ability to make good judgments (Civil Code, article 220).

As a general rule, you cannot make a valid **last will and testament** (a legal document in which you state who will get your property after you die) until you are a legal adult.

There are small exceptions to this rule in some provinces. In Newfoundland and Labrador, for example, you can make a will once you turn 17 (Wills Act, s. 3). In Québec, article 708 of the Civil Code says that, while, in general, a minor cannot make a will, he or she can do so for objects of little value (such as clothes or toys). Also, if you are married, if you join the Canadian Forces, or if you are a sailor at sea, you may be able to make a will regardless of your age, depending on provincial legislation.

Taking Legal Action

If you want to take someone to court, the law normally requires that an adult—variously referred to as a **litigation guardian,** a guardian *ad litem*, or a next friend—act in your place. Generally speaking, any adult can serve as a litigation guardian. This person could be a relative (such as a parent or an older brother or sister), an adult friend, or a lawyer who has been granted power of attorney (that is, the legal authority to act on another person's behalf). Even though a litigation guardian may actually *be* a lawyer, your litigation guardian is your stand-in, not your legal counsel. Instead, your litigation guardian will work with your lawyer, just as you would if you were old enough to act on your own behalf. If you're unable to find a litigation guardian yourself, you may be able to request that the court find someone for you.

There are some exceptions to the rule that you need a litigation guardian. In Ontario, for example, you may sue in Small Claims Court for a sum of up to $500 as if you were of full age (Ontario Regulation 258/98: Rules of the Small Claims Court, 4.01[2]). The rules about litigation guardians vary from province to province. Ontario sets these rules out in Regulation 194: Rules of Civil Procedure. Among other things, the regulation states that, while the litigation guardian can be any person "who is not under disability" (that is, any legally competent adult), that person must promise to fulfill certain duties, which include engaging a lawyer to represent the minor's case. If no litigation guardian can be found, the court may appoint the Children's Lawyer to serve in that role (in which case, unlike other litigation guardians, the Children's Lawyer will not be obliged to engage a lawyer).

In Québec, a minor who wants to start a lawsuit must generally be represented by a parent or other legal guardian, and the court action is brought in the guardian's name. With the court's permission, however, you may act alone in lawsuits concerning your legal status, the authority of your parents, and in certain other matters in which the law regards you as an adult (such as employment, as we mentioned above). In addition, if you believe that you have not been treated fairly because you lack adequate representation or because your status as a minor has placed you at a legal disadvantage, you may, in your own defence, bring this issue to the court's attention on your own (Civil Code, articles 159 and 160).

It is possible that you will want to sue someone. (This may happen, for instance, if you have entered into a contract and you believe that the other party has not honoured their obligations.) In that case, you or your litigation guardian go to court to tell the judge the reasons why the person you are suing should pay you money or do what you want. That person or their lawyer can argue why they should not have to pay you and may ask you hard questions to test if you are telling the truth. Depending on the case, it might be necessary to call witnesses to confirm what happened. Suing someone is very serious business, and you need to have good reasons and evidence to support your case. If possible, even if the law does not require it in your province, you should have a lawyer to help you by representing you in court or at least by giving you advice. A lawyer can be expensive; sometimes, however, you can get free representation, or at least advice, from legal clinics that help youth or underprivileged groups. (We provide links to some of these in appendix C.) We should note that we are talking here about *civil* court, which is where you go to get your rights enforced or to sue someone for damage that they caused you. We will talk about *criminal* court, where trials of people accused of crimes take place, in chapter 8.

Medical Decisions

Interestingly, although the law tends to limit the capacity of young people to make even relatively inconsequential decisions for themselves, when it comes to medical care, Canadian lawmakers and courts have seen fit to give at least *some* decision-making power to minors. Although, in the case of a younger child, it will generally be his or her parents or guardians who consent to or refuse medical treatment on the child's behalf, in most provinces and territories the child will have more power to make such decisions alone as he or she grows older and more mature. This is in large part thanks to *Gillick v. West Norfolk and Wisbech Health Authority,* a famous English case from 1985 which we will return to in chapter 3. It concerned the legal right of doctors to provide birth control to girls under 16 without parental consent, and the principles established in this case significantly influenced court decisions concerning medical consent of minors in other Commonwealth countries, including Canada.

In fact, you may not necessarily have to wait right up until the age of majority to have full power to make your own medical choices. In some provinces, the law allows everyone aged 16 or older to consent to medical treatment just as if they were adults, at least in most cases. In New Brunswick, for example, section 2 of the Medical Consent of Minors Act says that, once you turn 16, you have the same rights as an adult to consent to medical treatment. Section 3(1) then says that, if you are under 16, you may consent to medical treatment if, in the opinion of a medical practitioner, you are able to understand the nature and consequences of the treatment and it is in your best interests to receive such treatment.

In Québec, you may consent to treatment alone once you are 14 (Civil Code, article 14). If you are in need of medical care but are unable to give consent yourself and your parents refuse to do so, a court may order it. Similarly, if, once you are 14, you refuse medical care, you cannot be forced to have it without a court order—unless it is a serious emergency, in which case the consent of a parent or guardian is enough to override your will (Civil Code, article 16). However, until you turn 18 (the age of majority in Québec), you need your parents' written permission to decide whether you'd prefer to be buried or cremated and what kind of funeral you want to have. In other words, 14-year-olds have some decision-making power about health issues while they're still alive, but they need parental permission to have something done with their body once they are dead!

Rather than setting a minimum age of consent, some provinces instead use the rule that whether or not a young person can consent to his or her own medical care depends on his or her degree of maturity. In British Columbia, for instance, a doctor can give you medical care, including cosmetic treatments, without your parents' consent, provided that he or she (a) has explained the nature and consequences, as well as the benefits and risks, of the care and is satisfied that you understand them and (b) has concluded that the care is in your best interests (Infants Act, s. 17). Ontario's Health Care Consent Act, 1996 (s. 4) takes a similar approach. The idea that, as young people grow older and more mature, they should be given greater power to make their own decisions is often called the "mature minor" principle. (We will have more to say about this principle in the next chapter.)

When a province or territory allows minors to give legal consent to medical treatment, it normally also allows them to refuse it, provided the young person understands the consequences of the decision. However, if you refuse treatment, the courts can review your decision at your doctor's request. If, in the medical opinion of your doctor, receiving the treatment is very important to your health, he or she will very probably ask the court to name a guardian (such as provincial social services) to consent to the treatment on your behalf. The judge can choose to let you refuse the treatment, but the more serious the consequences of not receiving the recommended care, the less likely it is that a judge will want to declare you mature enough to refuse it.

This principle was illustrated in a well-known Supreme Court case, *A.C. v. Manitoba (Director of Child and Family Services)* (2009 SCC 30 [CanLII]). Section 25(8) of Manitoba's Child and Family Services Act allows a court to authorize a medical treatment for a child under 16 when it considers the treatment to be in a child's best interests. A Manitoba court had therefore forced life-saving blood transfusions on a 14-year-old Jehovah's Witness who had refused them for religious reasons. Her parents appealed on the grounds that Manitoba's law violated their daughter's rights under the Charter of Rights and Freedoms, but the Supreme Court upheld the Manitoba court's decision. The consensus was that, even though a team of hospital psychiatrists had judged the girl to be a mature minor, this didn't automatically give her the right to make all her own medical decisions. In a joint opinion, several of the justices argued that a "sliding scale of scrutiny" exists, "with the adolescent's views becoming increasingly determinative depending on his or her ability to exercise mature, independent judgment. The more serious the nature of the decision, and the more severe its potential impact on the life or health of the child, the greater the degree of scrutiny that will be required" (para. 22). In other words, despite the general rule that a young person's views acquire greater weight as he or she grows older, a court has more leeway to override those wishes in a life-and-death situation such as this one. In a dissenting opinion, one judge argued that since the girl had been found capable of making her own decisions, her wishes should be respected even if doing so was not in her best interests. But most judges will not want the responsibility of allowing a person that young to choose to die, even if he or she is clearly mature enough to make that decision in the same way as an adult.

Finally, in several situations, special rules apply:

- *Doctor-patient confidence.* In some provinces (Ontario, for example), you may be able to talk privately to a doctor about your health, and the doctor may be expected to keep the information you give him or her secret from your parents. Birth control is one example of a health concern that young people often want to keep private. However, the rules vary depending on where you live. We'll have more to say about this in chapter 6.

- *Being placed in a mental health facility.* If there is reason to believe that someone is mentally ill and could seriously harm himself or herself or someone else, that person can be declared incompetent and treated in a mental institution. In general, this is true both for young people and adults, but the younger you are, the more difficult it may be to appeal decisions about whether you are mentally incompetent.

- *Donating blood, organs, or tissue.* For health reasons, Canadian Blood Services require you to be at least 17 to donate blood. The age at which you can consent to donating a living organ for transplantation is 16 in Ontario and Prince Edward Island, 18 in Alberta, Manitoba, Saskatchewan, and Québec, and 19 everywhere else. There may be partial exceptions to this rule, as well as rules about donating organs after death. In Alberta, for instance, you can donate an organ before you are 18 if your parents agree and if certain strict conditions are met: that no one has coerced you into donating the organ, that there are no adult members of your immediate family who can be donors, and (until you are 16) that the tissue you are donating will replace itself. (For example, your body can produce more blood or bone marrow, but it can't regrow a kidney.) Manitoba has similar rules. In Québec, until you are 18, you may donate only a part of your body that can regrow itself and can safely be removed from your body, and only with the consent of your parents or guardians; however, once you are 14, you may sign consent for your organs to be donated after your death or for your body to be donated to science, without their permission.

Applying for Social Assistance (Welfare)

Social assistance (often called "welfare" or "income assist-ance") is money given by the provincial government to people who are temporarily or permanently unable to work and who do not have enough money from any other source (such as savings, property, or employment insurance) to support themselves. Parents who don't have enough money to support their family can usually apply for social assist-ance; if their application is approved, they will receive more money if they have children than they otherwise would. Parents raising children on a limited income are sometimes also given an income supplement such as the Canada child benefit, which is paid for partly by the federal government.

Social assistance is primarily given to adults, rather than to minors, as most minors are supported by their parents. However, depending on the province, you may be eligible for social assistance yourself at the age of 16 or 17—pos-sibly even before that under some conditions, typically if you are living apart from your parents. But the conditions for receiving assistance as a minor may be very strict. For example, consider Ontario's rules for allowing minors to participate in Ontario Works, that province's social assist-ance program. Before you are given social assistance, your parents have to be asked to provide support to you. If they refuse, you are required to go to court and sue your parents for support under section 31 of Ontario's Family Law Act, unless there are good reasons not to do so. If all of this fails, you may get assistance—if a number of other conditions are also met. Here are some of the main ones:

- You are 16 or over (a person under 16 who has to support someone else may qualify).

- You are attending school when obliged to do so.

- You cannot live with your parents because they have died, or have abandoned you, or are unable to provide adequate care or support *or* because "irreconcilable differences" (very serious disagreements or ongoing problems) exist between you that make it impossible for you to live together.

- The money will not be given to you directly but to a responsible adult who will manage it for your benefit.

Remember that social assistance is meant to cover only your very basic needs, and it is meant to end as soon as you are able to support yourself. The idea is that people who are able to support themselves should not be using public money, and so there are rules that can make it difficult to get social assistance. This makes sense to some extent, but it may also significantly limit the options of youth who find themselves in a crisis situation.

Are Age Restrictions Fair?

Perhaps some of the above age restrictions seem to you unjust. Indeed, section 15(1) of the Charter states:

> Every individual is equal before and under the law and has the right to the equal protection and equal benefit of the law without discrimination and, in

particular, without discrimination based on race,
national or ethnic origin, colour, religion, sex, age
or mental or physical disability.

In other words, the law should apply equally to everybody and shouldn't discriminate against certain people just
because of their age.

The rights and freedoms laid out in the Charter are not
unlimited, however. According to section 1, these rights and
freedoms are "subject only to such reasonable limits prescribed by law as can be demonstrably justified in a free and
democratic society." This means that the law can place limits
on these rights and freedoms, provided most people agree
that these limits make good sense—that they are "demonstrably justified." For example, most adults still believe that
banning people under the age of 18 from voting puts a reasonable limit on their rights. So, while you may think that
many of the laws restricting your rights because of your age
are unreasonable and undemocratic, the problem is that no
one has yet convinced the courts of this. Moreover, as you've
probably noticed, laws are made by adults.

As this chapter illustrates, although the law allows you to
make decisions about some things even while you are still a
minor, when all is said and done, these things are somewhat
limited. In fact, even the situations in which adults must
ask for your opinion and take it into consideration before
making a decision about you are rather limited. Yet article 12
of the Convention on the Rights of the Child says that a child
who is old enough to form his or her own views has "the

right to express those views freely in all matters affecting the child" and that these views should be "given due weight in accordance with the age and maturity of the child."

As it stands, except perhaps in relation to medical decisions, Canadian law still does relatively little to uphold this right. Of course, age restrictions are often meant for your own protection. But young people obviously mature at different rates, and nothing magical happens the moment you turn 18 or 19. In many cases, though, the law doesn't even give you a chance to try to prove that you are mature enough to do something that someone of your age is normally not allowed to do. In practical terms, it makes sense to set age limits that are the same for all young people. But we can't help wondering what alternative approaches could be found. Where firm age restrictions *are* found to be necessary, perhaps the law could do more to encourage (or even oblige) parents and other adults to consult with children before making decisions on their behalf.

BEING YOUR PARENTS' CHILD

Your relationship with your parents is one of the most important you will ever have, but it is not always an easy relationship. Young people want love from their parents. They expect their parents to provide them with physical care and emotional support—to listen to them, to understand their needs, and to be proud of their accomplishments. Most parents try to take good care of their children and are happy when their children are happy. At the same time, while some are stricter than others, parents generally expect their children to obey them. Some insist that their children simply do what they say and not talk back or even ask questions, while others are more willing to listen to their children's points of view and have discussions. But even though parents generally mean well, they don't always know how best to act on their good intentions. Some parents may be overwhelmed with problems that leave them little energy for their children, while, sadly, others are simply uncaring. They may be immature and selfish—more interested in their own emotional needs than in those of their children.

Your relationship to your parents is a personal, private one, but it's also a legal one, which largely falls under a branch of the law known as *family law*. As we mentioned at the start of this book, the law once gave parents, especially fathers, a great many rights over their children but very few responsibilities toward them. In essence, the law viewed children as the personal property of their parents, to do with what they wished. But the law no longer upholds this attitude. A good example is the Supreme Court decision in *B. (R.) v. Children's Aid Society of Metropolitan Toronto* (1995 CanLII 115 [SCC]), a case that involved an infant, born prematurely with a number of medical problems, who had received a blood transfusion against her parents' wishes. In deciding that the parents had no legal grounds for complaint, the justices explicitly stated in several places that children are not property. For example, the chief justice wrote that the freedom of parents to make decisions on behalf of their children "is not a parental right tantamount to a right of property in children" (372).[1]

---

1 He added, in parentheses: "Fortunately, we have distanced ourselves from the ancient juridical conception of children as chattels of their parents" (372). (A "chattel" is a personal possession.) Two of the other justices likewise stated: "The suggestion that parents have the ability to refuse their children medical procedures such as blood transfusions in situations where such a transfusion is necessary to sustain that child's health is consistent with the view, *now long gone*, that parents have some sort of 'property interest' in their children" (432–433, our emphasis).

But this case is important for another reason. In deciding against the parents, the Court argued that, in exercising their power to make decisions, parents must act in accordance with a child's best interests. As the two justices just quoted went on to say: "The nature of the parent-child relationship is thus not to be determined by the personal desires of the parent, yet rather by the 'best interests' of the child." Precisely what a child's "best interests" are will vary depending on the situation, but the general idea is that parents or guardians should be attentive to a child's physical, mental, and emotional needs and cannot make decisions that would in some way harm the child or undermine his or her chances of developing normally into an adult.

The Supreme Court had already explored the concept of a child's "best interests" in *Young v. Young* (1993 CanLII 34 [SCC]), a case that involved a dispute over child custody. As one of the justices aptly put it, "The child has a right to a parent who will look after his or her best interests and the custodial parent a duty to ensure, protect and promote the child's best interests" (5). The "best interests" principle is also spelled out in a number of provincial statutes. For example, section 20(2) of Ontario's Children's Law Reform Act says that someone entitled to the custody of a child has the rights and responsibilities of a parent and "must exercise those rights and responsibilities in the best interests of the child." And Ontario's Child, Youth and Family Services Act, 2017 opens by saying, in section 1(1): "The paramount purpose of this Act is to promote the best interests, protection and well-being of children." Section 74(3) then describes the factors that should be considered when one is trying to determine a child's best interests.

The "best interests" principle gives young people an important legal safeguard against parental abuse. All the same, how parents choose to raise their children has traditionally been seen as a private matter, one in which the law should not meddle—and the law is still reluctant to interfere in family matters, except when a specific issue is brought to court. At the same time, it does have quite a lot to say about the parent-child relationship in general. So let's have a look at the rights and responsibilities that the law gives to parents and to children, as well as what things it makes rules about and what things it leaves to people to decide for themselves.

Parental Support

Historically, parents' legal duty to support their children has included only the "necessaries of life"—adequate food, clothing, and shelter. By and large, this is still the law today. Although parents are required to provide for their children to the extent that they are able to do so, their duty is to supply your basic needs, not your wants. In other words, children are not entitled to luxuries, unless a court specifically decides otherwise. For example, in a divorce, the parent who is awarded custody of a child may be able to establish that it is in the best interests of the child (or children) to continue going to a private school, for instance, or to continue with elite gymnastics training, because that is what the children are used to. (This happened in one of Marvin's cases as a family court judge.) In such a case, the judge may order the other parent to pay the amount of child support that will cover these things.

 Do I have the right to live with my parents?

Suppose your parents want to send you away to live with relatives. Is there anything you can do about it? In general, the law leaves such decisions up to parents. As we have seen, it requires only that parents not place their child at a risk of harm and that they act in the child's best interests. So, for example, if your parents felt confident that your grandparents would take good care of you and that living with them would actually be more to your advantage than staying at home, they could decide to send you to live with them. But this would probably be a hard choice for many parents to have to make, and it wouldn't necessarily mean simply that they don't love you.

It's also possible for parents to place their children in the care of the state. The rules for doing so vary from one province to another, so it may be easier for parents to give their children over to the care of the state in some places and situations than in others. In Ontario, for example, people who are temporarily unable to take care of their child—as might happen if they face a medical or financial emergency, for instance—may make an agreement with a children's aid society to take their child into its care (Child, Youth and

Family Services Act, 2017, s. 75[1]). If there is somewhere better for the child to live temporarily *and* the agency finds that there is no other solution that is less disruptive, such as care in the child's own home, the agency may take the child into its care—although, from the age of 12, the child will normally be allowed to participate in the agreement (ss. 75[2] and 75[4]). This is only in the case of temporary care, which should generally last no more than six months and is meant to end with the child returning to the parents. Sometimes, though, conditions in the family may be such that parents will be unfit to take care of their child for a long time, which in extreme cases can result in the child's ending up in the permanent care of the state. This is actually an important topic on its own. We talk about what happens when parents are unable or unwilling to take care of their children in more detail in chapter 7, which is about child protection.

In some circumstances, parents may choose to end their relationship with a child by arranging for the child to be adopted by another person. This usually happens while the child is still a baby. Most often, parents choose adoption because they did not plan for the mother to get pregnant and don't feel ready or able to raise a child. Adoption makes it possible for the baby to be raised in a family that wants a child and will give him or her love and good care. While it's also possible for parents to give older children up for adoption, this is not common, and when it happens it's usually because of some very serious issues in the family.

Giving your child up for adoption is not a simple matter of handing a child over to another person. Adoptions are typically approved by the courts and overseen either by a government agency or by a private adoption agency. In either case, the agency will try to have the child placed in a home that seems right for him or her—although, in the end, parents reserve the legal right to consent to the adoption. If a child is permanently in the care of the state, however, the parents' consent is not necessary for an adoption: in that situation, the province or territory is the child's legal guardian. Also, if the child has reached a certain age, his or her consent may be required before an adoption can be approved. In most of Canada that age is 12, but it can be as low as 7 (in Ontario) and as high as 14 (in Québec—where, however, a child aged 10 or more may refuse to consent, although a court can override his or her wishes). In some jurisdictions, the law allows for exceptions to the age rule if a court decides that allowing a child to give or refuse consent would not be in that child's best interests. So, for example, a young person's consent to adoption might not be required if, in the opinion of a judge, he or she is not mentally able to understand the situation.

Once you are adopted, you are now, in the eyes of the law, the child of your adoptive parents. All the parental rights and responsibilities of your biological parents end and pass to your adoptive parents, while any legal rights and obligations you might otherwise have had with your biological parents, such as rights to inheritance, end as well.

Q How long do my parents have to support me? Is it true that they can kick me out of the house when I turn 16?

There is a good deal of confusing, and often incomplete, information out there about this question. As we have said above, parents have a legal duty to support their children. This duty *does not* end at the age of 16: every single province and territory in Canada requires parents to support their children at least until the age of majority.

One possible source of confusion about how long young people are entitled to parental support has to do with paragraph 215(1)(a) of the Criminal Code, which, under the heading "Duties Tending to Preservation of Life," says that a parent or other guardian must provide the "necessaries of life" for *a child under the age of 16*. This means that, up to the point at which a child turns 16, a parent or guardian who fails to provide such necessities is guilty of a crime and can be arrested and put in prison. The paragraph does *not* say that the duty of parents to support their children ends at the age of 16; it means only that, once a child has reached the age of 16, a parent who fails to provide support cannot be charged with a crime on that account.[2]

---

2 In fact, in certain circumstances, such a parent *could* be charged with a crime. The same subsection of the Criminal Code goes on to say, in paragraph (c), that all people have a legal duty to provide the necessaries of life to a person under their charge "if that person (i) is unable, by reason of detention, age, illness, mental disorder, or other cause, to withdraw himself [or herself] from that charge, and (ii) is unable to provide himself [or herself] with necessaries of life." So, for example, a parent could be charged with a crime for failing to provide support to an older child who is too badly disabled to manage on his or her own.

Under family law, however, which is mainly a provincial or territorial responsibility, parental support obligations ordinarily last at least until the local age of majority and can actually continue past that age, mainly if the child is still enrolled in a full-time educational program (high school, college, or university) or is too sick or disabled to leave his or her parents' care (see table 1). Parents who refuse to perform these duties can be taken to court by their children and sued for support.

Table 1 Duration of the right to parental support

How long a parent is obliged to provide support	Relevant legal provision(s)
Alberta. Until 18; until 22 if the child is under the parent's charge and studying full-time	Family Law Act, ss. 46(b) and 49(1)
British Columbia. Until 19; longer if the child is unable, because of illness, disability, or another reason, to obtain the necessaries of life or withdraw from the parent's charge	Family Law Act, ss. 146 and 147(1)
Manitoba. Until 18; longer if the child is unable, by reason of illness, disability, or other cause, to withdraw from the parent's charge or obtain the necessaries of life	Family Maintenance Act, ss. 35.1 and 36(1)
New Brunswick. Until 19; longer if the child is unable to withdraw from the parent's charge or to obtain the necessaries of life by reason of illness, disability, pursuit of reasonable education, or other cause	Family Services Act, s. 113(1)

How long a parent is obliged to provide support	Relevant legal provision(s)
Newfoundland and Labrador. Until 19; longer if the child is under the parent's charge and is unable, by reason of illness, disability, pursuit of reasonable education, or other cause, to withdraw from the parent's charge or to obtain the necessities of life	Family Law Act, section 37
Northwest Territories. Until 19; longer if the child is unable, by reason of illness, disability, pursuit of reasonable education, or other cause, to withdraw from the parent's charge	Children's Law Act, sections 57 and 58
Nova Scotia. Until 19; court may order support for a child older than 19 who is unable, by reason of illness, disability, or other cause, to withdraw from the parent's charge or obtain the necessaries of life	Parenting and Support Act (formerly the Maintenance and Custody Act), ss. 2(c), 8, and 9
Nunavut. Until 19; longer if the child is unable, by reason of illness, disability, pursuit of reasonable education, or other cause, to withdraw from the parent's charge	Children's Law Act, ss. 57 and 58
Ontario. Until 18; longer if the child is studying full-time or is unable, by reason of illness, disability, or other cause, to withdraw from the parent's charge	Family Law Act, s. 31(1)

How long a parent is obliged to provide support	Relevant legal provision(s)
Prince Edward Island. Until 18; longer if the child is studying full-time or unable to withdraw from the parent's charge or to obtain the necessaries of life	Family Law Act, s. 31(1)
Québec. Until 18; in addition, an adult child who is in need deserves basic forms of support from his or her immediate family	Civil Code of Québec, articles 585, 587, and 599, para. 2
Saskatchewan. Until 18; longer if the child is unable, by reason of illness, disability, pursuit of reasonable education, or other cause, to withdraw from the parent's charge or obtain the necessaries of life	Family Maintenance Act, 1997, ss. 3 and 4
Yukon. Until 19; longer if the child is under the parent's charge and is unable by reason of illness, disability, or other cause to withdraw from parent's charge or obtain the necessaries of life	Family Property and Support Act, ss. 1 and 32

At the same time, the law generally places certain restrictions on the right of older children to parental support. By way of a fairly typical example, here is what section 31 of the Ontario Family Law Act says about parental support:

Obligation of parent to support child

31 (1) Every parent has an obligation to provide support, to the extent that the parent is capable of doing so, for his or her unmarried child who,

(a) is a minor;

(b) is enrolled in a full-time program of education; or

(c) is unable by reason of illness, disability or other cause to withdraw from the charge of his or her parents.

Same

(2) The obligation under subsection (1) does not extend to a child who is sixteen years of age or older and has withdrawn from parental control.

According to the first subsection, a young person who is studying full-time or who cannot reasonably be expected to care for himself or herself is entitled to parental support even if he or she is no longer a minor.[3] But this rule ceases to apply if the young person gets married. The second subsection then says that a young person also loses this entitlement if, at any point after turning 16, he or she is considered to have "withdrawn from parental control." This basically means that the young person has left home of his or her own free will and/or has chosen to reject parental authority in order to live an independent life.

As we will see below, many provinces and territories allow young people to leave home before they reach the age of majority. Yet, except in Québec, no formal procedure

---

3 In a case that recently came before the Ontario Court of Justice, the judge ruled that the obligation to provide continued support extends to both parents if the two have divorced. In this decision, the father of a 24-year-old disabled man, who was now living with his mother, was ordered to keep paying child support. See *Coates v. Watson* (2017 ONCJ 454 [CanLII]) and *Coates v. Watson* (2018 ONCJ 605 [CanLII]).

exists for withdrawing from parental control, nor do statutes such as Ontario's Family Law Act explicitly define the term. In cases where a question has arisen about whether parents still owe support to a child who has withdrawn from their control, judges have generally ruled in favour of the young person when he or she had little choice but to leave home—when he or she had been kicked out of the house, or had left home to avoid abuse, or had left because the parents were imposing unreasonable rules and restrictions (although it's up to a judge to decide what qualifies as unreasonable). If leaving home was not a voluntary decision, then the child still has a right to parental support. In a case recently decided in Ontario, for example, a 17-year-old girl whose parents had divorced many years earlier succeeded in withdrawing from her father's control against his wishes. Her father, with whom she had been living, had been behaving in a domineering manner and was trying to prevent her from seeing her mother and from enrolling at a university in Florida, where her mother (who had remarried) now lived. The girl argued that her father's controlling nature and arbitrary rules made living in his home unbearable and that her withdrawal was therefore involuntary, in which case she was still entitled to support. The courts agreed: her request for an official declaration of withdrawal was granted, and she was able to get a court order for parental support during her studies.[4]

---

4 See *R.G. v. K.G.* (2017 ONCA 108 [CanLII]), regarding the declaration of withdrawal, and *O.G. v. R.G.* (2017 ONCJ 153 [CanLII]), for the decision about support.

That said, judges may also choose to limit the amount of support you are entitled to receive, usually by factoring in your relative ability to earn money to support yourself, while perhaps also taking your family's overall financial situation into consideration. For example, if you are attending a university or college, a judge might order your parents to pay you a certain amount each month but at the same time instruct you to contribute to your own support by finding a summer job.

Do these support obligations mean that your parents can't kick you out of the house until you finish your studies? You might think that as long as your parents still have the duty to support you, they should be obliged to allow you to live at home. However, the law does not say that supporting a child requires parents to allow that child to live in their own home. Perhaps because, once a child turns 16, it is no longer a federal crime to fail to provide support, parents may just decide that they can treat their child the same way as a trespasser on their property. According to standard laws about trespassing, if someone asks a person to leave their property and the trespasser refuses, the property owner can use reasonable force to remove the person or else call the police, who can come and remove the trespasser themselves. (In some jurisdictions, the trespasser can also be arrested and punished.) Ultimately, what will happen to a youth over 16 whose parents wish to kick him or her out will largely depend on provincial or territorial laws. In Saskatchewan child welfare agencies cannot legally take a young person who is 16 or older into their care, and the law may also restrict the range of services that are available after that age. (We'll have more to say about these restrictions in chapter 7.) In addition, what will happen to such a youth may depend on how the police choose to enforce the existing laws. Provided that this is an option, the police may simply decide to take the young person to the local child welfare authorities. Or they might refuse to intervene in the situation without a court order—or they might just help the parents turn their child out of the house. In this last case, the young person has the right to remove his or her personal possessions from the home, and the police may be willing to take the youth to a homeless shelter or to the home of a friend or relative who has agreed to take him or her in. At that point, the youth can turn to the child welfare authorities for whatever help they are able to provide.

Regardless of exactly what happens, though, *a youth who has been evicted from home should promptly file a claim for support in the local court.* Assuming that the youth is eligible for support under provincial law, the judge will order the parents to provide that support and will determine its amount. If the parents remain unwilling to let their teenage child live with them, they will have to cover the cost of alternative accommodation (such as an apartment). Living on the streets, even temporarily, is *extremely* dangerous, as it leaves a young person vulnerable to all kinds of violence and exploitation. So a youth in this situation should go to court to request support and stay in a shelter or, if possible, with someone who can be trusted while waiting for the court to order the support.

A Case of Good Fortune

In a case tried in Alberta—*R. v. R.D.* (2005 ABPC 54 [CanLII])—a 16-year-old boy had been living on the streets after his father kicked him out. One day, a neighbour spotted him breaking into the family home through a window and leaving with a plastic bag, which turned out to contain grocery items. The boy was arrested and charged with breaking and entering and with theft, and he was also handed over to the child welfare authorities, who gave him shelter in a group home. At his trial, the judge, Danielle Dalton, examined the relevant laws, including several articles of the Convention on the Rights of the Child. As she pointed out, because the boy had not withdrawn voluntarily from the family home, his father still had a duty to support him, and yet his father had not found him another place to live or otherwise supplied his needs. She therefore concluded that the boy had a right to be in his father's house and eat food from it, and so she found him not guilty.

This boy was fortunate to have a sympathetic judge, and her decision sets a useful precedent, one that judges in other provinces could draw on. All the same, a court in another province could well decide to convict a youth who did the same thing—and there are cases where such convictions have occurred. So, should you ever find yourself in this situation, we don't recommend breaking and entering. Rather, you should try to get help through the child welfare authorities and ask a court to order your parents to support you.

To summarize, then: as a general rule, parents in Canada have the duty to support their children at least until they are of legal age, and in some circumstances even longer. However, once their child reaches the age of 16, parents may be able to avoid fulfilling this duty until a court, at the young person's request, orders them to do so. A youth who is 16 or older may thus have to put up with being kicked out and will then have to go to court in order to obtain further support from his or her parents.

With all this in mind, we think that the law could do a better job of safeguarding your right to safety and shelter: under no circumstances should a young person be forced out into the street on short notice. A landlord cannot even legally do this to a tenant who fails to pay rent, so why should parents be able to do this to their own child? In our view, parents should not have the right to drive a teenage child out on a whim, even if the youth can subsequently apply to the court for financial support. Rather, parents should be legally obliged to provide their children with a safe place to live at least until they reach the age of majority. If, for some reason, parents would strongly prefer that an older child leave their home, then they should be required to rent an apartment or otherwise arrange for acceptable accommodation *before* the child moves out and to provide their child with a reasonable living allowance until he or she is in a position to be self-supporting. Leaving your parents' home is a major turning point in your life, and, rather than abruptly evicting you, your parents should be obliged to help you prepare to take this step.

Parental Authority

It should be clear by now that the law gives parents a great deal of power over their children. But just how much power? Must you always do what your parents tell you to do? Do you have any right to make your own decisions, or is it entirely up to your parents to decide whether to give you a voice? This is an important question, although not one that has a simple answer.

In practical terms, the extent of parents' power over their children largely depends on how a court judge interprets the relevant laws in relation to a specific situation. These laws could include federal ones, such as the Divorce Act or even the Charter of Rights and Freedoms, but they are often provincial or territorial laws. In addition, other than in Québec, judges are also guided by common law precedents. Bear with us, then, while we provide a bit of background to this issue.

For a very long time, English common law assumed that parental authority over their children was virtually absolute. As we mentioned earlier, children were basically regarded as their parents' possessions. Gradually, however, people began to question this view, which was challenged on several occasions in court. Finally, in 1985, a case came before the highest court of appeal in the land—which, at the time, was the British House of Lords.[5] The

---

5 Until fairly recently, the House of Lords retained a judicial function, in addition to its more familiar legislative one. In 2009, this judicial function was transferred to the newly created Supreme Court of the United Kingdom.

case, *Gillick v. West Norfolk and Wisbech Area Health Authority,* involved the right of girls under the age of 16 to decide for themselves about the use of contraception. In a 3-to-2 majority in their favour, the judges ruled that parental authority was *not* absolute but gradually dwindled as the child became more mature. In the words of one of the judges, Lord Scarman, "parental right yields to the child's right to make his [or her] own decisions when he [or she] reaches a sufficient understanding and intelligence to be capable of making up his [or her] own mind on the matter requiring decision" ([1985] 3 All E.R. 402 [H.L.] at 422). As a result, the law of England no longer considers that parents have the right to require absolute obedience from their children. Instead, the courts will support the child's right to make his or her own decisions if the child is judged to be mature enough to do so.

But that's England. Can the same thing be said of Canadian law? As we saw in the previous chapter, the "mature minor" principle—that young people should be given greater capacity for independent decision making as they grow older and more mature—is not unknown in Canada, especially in relation to medical decisions. In fact, just a year after the *Gillick* case was decided, an Alberta Court of Appeal judge drew on that ruling in *J.S.C. v. Wren* (1986 ABCA 249 [CanLII]), a case that involved a 16-year-old girl's decision to have an abortion. In dismissing her parents' appeal, the judge wrote: "Parental rights (and obligations) clearly do exist, and they do not wholly disappear until the age of majority. The modern law, however, is that the courts will exercise increasing restraint in that regard as a child grows to and through adolescence. The law and the development of the law in this respect was analyzed in detail by Lord Scarman in the *Gillick* case" (para. 13). He went on to quote Lord Scarman's conclusion that "the parental right to determine whether or not their minor child below the age of 16 will have medical treatment terminates if and when the child achieves a sufficient understanding and intelligence to enable him or her to understand fully what is proposed" (qtd. in para. 14).

In Alberta case law, then, there is some support for the principle laid out in the *Gillick* decision, at least with regard to medical matters. But what about our highest court—the Supreme Court of Canada? Let's return to *A.C. v. Manitoba (Director of Child and Family Services)* (2009 SCC 30 [CanLII]), in which the Supreme Court examined the "mature minor" principle in relation to a 14-year-old girl's right to refuse a medically necessary blood transfusion. In so doing, the Court carefully considered the *Gillick* decision, including its history of legal application (paras. 48–79). Yet, in the end, while acknowledging the importance of the principle, the justices chose to limit its scope by allowing courts to override a mature minor's wishes in relatively serious medical circumstances, if the court feels that what the young person wants is not in his or her best interests. In a dissenting opinion, however, one judge argued that, because the girl had been found to be capable of making her own decisions, her wishes should have been respected even if the result was not in her best interests.[6]

By now, you're probably wondering what all this has to do with parental authority. In England, the *Gillick* decision established a general principle by which parents should be guided in raising their children—namely, that parents must give their child greater power to make independent decisions as that child's understanding and ability to exercise judgment increases with age. This view emphasizes a young person's growing *capacity*. In Canada, this principle has been upheld only in specific contexts (notably in connection with medical care)—and, as the decision in *A.C. v. Manitoba* indicates, when it comes to very serious matters, such as life-and-death situations, the "best interests" principle trumps not only parental views and preferences but also those of an otherwise mature minor. This perspective places greater emphasis on a young person's need for *protection* and helps to explain why, in Canada, how much power parents have to deny their children the right to make independent decisions is generally left up to judges who are considering specific situations. Except in Québec (which relies on its Civil Code in family matters), the scope of

6 Interestingly, six years earlier, in *Starson v. Swayze* (2003 SCC 32 [CanLII]), the Supreme Court had considered the case of an adult male who had been diagnosed with mental illness and whose capacity for decision making had been called into question. In this case, the Court upheld the right of the man to refuse treatment, even though doing so was arguably not in his best interests. But it proved unwilling to apply the same principle in the case of a mature minor whose refusal put her at risk of death.

parental authority is largely determined by the common law tradition. So far, only three provinces—one of them Québec—have, to any extent, attempted to spell out in their statutes the powers that parents have over their children. Here's what these three provinces have to say on the subject:

Alberta

Section 21(6) of the Family Law Act lists the powers that guardians (including parents) may exercise over a child. The list (which contains thirteen items in all) begins:

(a) to make day-to-day decisions affecting the child, including having the day-to-day care and control of the child and supervising the child's daily activities;

(b) to decide the child's place of residence and to change the child's place of residence;

(c) to make decisions about the child's education, including the nature, extent and place of education and any participation in extra-curricular school activities;

(d) to make decisions regarding the child's cultural, linguistic, religious and spiritual upbringing and heritage;

(e) to decide with whom the child is to live and with whom the child is to associate;

(f) to decide whether the child should work and, if so, the nature and extent of the work,

for whom the work is to be done and related
matters;

(g) to consent to medical, dental and other
health-related treatment for the child.

As you can see even from this partial list,
section 21(6) gives considerable powers to parents
or other guardians—although these powers are
limited in three important ways. First, section 21(1)
of the same act states that parents and other guardians must "exercise the powers, responsibilities and
entitlements of guardianship in the best interests of the child." (What counts as a child's "best
interests" is described in section 18[2].) Second,
section 21(6) itself opens with the words, "Except
where otherwise limited by law." This means that,
in exercising their powers over a child, parents or
guardians must abide by other laws. With regard
to school, for example, a parent could not make
decisions that violate the rules about school attendance laid out in Alberta's School Act. Similarly, in
deciding whether a child should work, a parent
must respect the provincial Employment Standards
Code, which contains rules about child labour.

Finally, subsection (7) goes on to say: "A guardian who exercises any of the powers referred to in
subsection (6) shall do so in a manner consistent
with the evolving capacity of the child." This is, in
essence, the *Gillick* principle—that as children grow
more mature (that is, as their capacity evolves),

their parents' authority over them should diminish accordingly. The Alberta Court of Appeal applied this rule in *MacKinnon v. Harrison* (2011 ABCA 283 [CanLII]). The case involved a 16-year-old girl whose divorced parents—one of whom had moved to British Columbia—disagreed about where she should live and where she should go to school. In ruling in favour of the girl's own wishes, the judge referred to the principle established in Britain in the *Gillick* case and concluded that the girl was mature enough to make her own decisions about where to live and go to school.

British Columbia

Section 41 of the BC Family Law Act has a list of "parental responsibilities," which are similar to the powers listed in Alberta's Family Law Act. However, the BC act does *not* include all the same three limits: there is only the requirement, stated in section 43(1), that parents should exercise their responsibilities in the child's best interests. On the subject of whether, in exercising their responsibilities, parents should gradually allow their children more room for independence, the BC act says nothing, one way or another.[7] Note, however,

---

7 In a 1986 ruling by the BC Superior Court—*Gareau v. B.C. (Supt. of Fam. & Child Services)* (1986 CanLII 1046 [BCSC])—the judge referred to the *Gillick* decision (made in Britain the previous year): "As to the question of when a person under the age of majority can decide things for himself or herself: see *Gillick v. West Norfolk & Wisbech Area Health*

that the act also bans "family violence"; this is
defined in section 1 to include, among other things,
"unreasonable restrictions on, or prevention of, a
family member's financial or personal autonomy."[8]

Québec

As we've explained, when it comes to civil matters,
Québec doesn't rely on common law but instead
on its Civil Code—so it would make sense that
Québec might have statutes that relate to parental
authority. The Civil Code does indeed address the
topic, although it doesn't say anything very specific.
According to article 597, "Every child, regardless of
age, owes respect to his father and mother." Articles
598 and 599 go on to say that "a child remains subject to the authority of his father and mother until

Authority, [1985] 3 All E.R. 402 (H.L.)." However, this comment, which
was enclosed in parentheses, was in the nature of an aside. The judge
was arguing that a family advocate isn't obliged to take instructions
from children "even if they are of an age of sufficient maturity to give
instructions." This statement does recognize that, at some point, children are mature enough to make their own choices, even though the
judge felt that this principle didn't apply in the present situation.

8 In 2019, the BC Supreme Court released a judgment where a
14-year-old transgender boy, "A.B.," was judged capable of consenting
to hormone therapy in order to transition to his preferred gender,
despite his father's objections. The judge also permitted A.B. to apply
to legally change his name and gender without parental consent and
ruled that attempting to persuade A.B. to abandon treatment for
gender dysphoria would be considered family violence under s. 38 of
the BC Family Law Act, as would addressing A.B. by his birth name
and referring to him as a girl or with female pronouns. See A.B. v. C.D.
and E.F., 2019 BCSC 254.

his majority or emancipation" and that "the father and mother have the rights and duties of custody, supervision and education of their children."

While the Civil Code clearly affirms that parents have authority over their children, it doesn't explicitly state that this authority is absolute. In fact, article 159 allows a minor to bring a court action "relating to his status, to the exercise of parental authority or to an act that he may perform alone." In other words, Québec law recognizes that young people may have reason to challenge their parents' right to make decisions on their behalf— but, as is the case elsewhere in Canada, the final decision rests in the hands of a judge.

From a purely practical point of view, there is nothing to stop parents, at a given moment in time, from enforcing whatever rules they see fit—although the authorities can intervene if they break the law or do anything that qualifies as child abuse or neglect. Short of leaving home, however, the only way in which a young person might successfully challenge a parent's rules is to take the parent to court over some issue, in hopes that the court will order the parent to respect his or her wishes in the matter. While it is certainly not impossible to take your own parents to court, it's a pretty extreme step, and not a particularly easy one. As we explained in chapter 2, you would possibly need an adult, such as a lawyer, a grown family member, or some other person (a "litigation guardian") who would be willing to represent you in court, depending on your province's rules for minors bringing a family case to court.

As we saw just above, in Québec, article 159 of the Civil Code allows you, *with the permission of the court,* to start a court action *without* an adult guardian in which you challenge your parents' exercise of their authority over you. This happened in a well-known case, *Droit de la famille 081485* (2008 QCCS 2709 [CanLII]), when the father of a 12-year-old girl, whose parents were separated, punished her by forbidding her to go on a school trip to Québec City. The girl's mother wanted to let her go on the trip, but she needed to have the permission of both her parents. So the girl took the case to court. After considering the circumstances, the judge concluded that the girl had already been punished once, by not being allowed to participate in a school show, and that the trip was educational and in her best interests. Therefore, the judge ordered that she be allowed to go on the trip.

Taking your parents to court to get more freedom may be possible, but we recommend that you do so only for a very good reason and that you think hard about the possible consequences. The father of the girl mentioned above was, for example, very angry that the court had ruled in favour of his daughter, who was now living with her mother, and said afterward that he would not speak with her until she was willing to accept his authority. So, before you take such a drastic action, it would be best to consult with a lawyer— preferably one who has experience helping young people cope with family issues.

> **Q** Can I leave home or otherwise end my parents' control over me before I reach the age of majority?

Yes, although this depends on your age and on where you live. If living at home becomes intolerable for you, it may be possible for another person to get a custody or guardianship order from a court that will allow you to live with them instead. You can also leave home voluntarily by withdrawing from parental control or, in Québec, by a process known as **emancipation**. So let's have a closer look at these options.

Custody and Guardianship Orders

It is generally possible for other people to ask a court to give them full custody or guardianship of a child or else to give them the power to make certain decisions about the child. As you might guess, the rules about who is eligible to apply for custody or guardianship vary from one province or territory to another—as does the use of these two terms.[9] In Ontario, for example, section 21(1) of the Children's Law Reform Act says that *any* person—an aunt or uncle, for example, or an adult whom the child trusts—may

---

9 The terms *custody* and *guardianship* are often used to mean basically the same thing, although some laws make a distinction between the two in terms of the kind of rights over a child that someone has. We tend to think of "custody" as something that a parent has, whereas we tend to think of a "guardian" as someone other than one of a child's biological parents. But this isn't necessarily accurate. A parent may or may not be a child's legal guardian, while, depending on the terminology used in a specific law, someone who is not one of the child's parents may be granted custody of the child.

apply in court for custody of a child or for the power to make decisions for the child about certain matters (what the law calls "incidents of custody"). Although, in some jurisdictions, this person must be a legal adult, the Ontario law does not, in principle, rule out the possibility that an older minor could apply for custody. In practice, however, a court would probably want the minor to be a close relative of the child (such as an older brother or sister) and would think long and hard before taking such a step. As a general rule, in deciding whether to grant custody to a person other than the child's parents, a court will be guided by its assessment of the child's best interests.

If you are frequently in conflict with your parents because of their rules, and you know of someone who would be willing to apply for your custody or guardianship, this could be an option. However, courts are generally reluctant to separate children from their parents unless no reasonable alternative can be found. So, for the person's application to be successful, a court would probably need to be convinced that these conflicts are serious and unlikely to be resolved and that the living situation at home genuinely is unhealthy for you. In cases of abuse or neglect, it might be social services who apply to take the young person into their care (see chapter 7).

Leaving Home Voluntarily

In most provinces and territories, the law allows an older minor to leave home voluntarily and thus to withdraw from parental control, whether or not his or her parents agree with this decision—although, to do this, a minor must generally be at least 16. In a few provinces, however, as well as in Yukon, the law requires youth to stay at home until they are legally adults, and those who leave before that are considered runaways. A runaway can be apprehended by the police and brought back home (or perhaps handed over to child welfare authorities)—although, in the case of older teenagers, the police may choose not to make a great effort to enforce this law. And, in some provinces, the authorities may intervene only if there is reason to believe that the runaway is in danger of coming to harm or if the parents get a court order. In table 2, we summarize what provincial and territorial laws have to say about the age at which you can legally leave home.

Table 2 Minimum age for legally leaving home

Age at which a minor may leave home	Relevant legal provision(s)
Alberta. At 16 to 18, depending on the circumstances	Possibility to leave before 18 implied by Family Law Act, s. 49(2)(b) and (at least for 16-year-olds) by s. 57.2(1)(a) of the Child, Youth and Family Enhancement Act; somewhat restricted by the same act, as in section 19(12)

Age at which a minor may leave home	Relevant legal provision(s)
British Columbia. At 19, with possible exceptions	Child, Family and Community Service Act, sections 26 and 27 (note the exception given by section 26[5]); s. 147(1)(b) of the Family Law Act seems to suggest that children may sometimes leave parents' care at an earlier age; other legal provisions may also apply
Manitoba. Generally at 18	Child and Family Services Act, ss. 1(1), 17(2)(a) and (d), and 21(1) and 21(3)
New Brunswick. Generally at 16	Family Services Act, ss. 29.2 and 31(5) and 31(6)
Newfoundland and Labrador. At 16	Children's Law Act, s. 73
Northwest Territories. At 16	Children's Law Act, s. 56
Nova Scotia. At 16 (may be extended to 19 if child is in care)	Children and Family Services Act, s. 29(4)
Nunavut. At 16	Children's Law Act, s. 56
Ontario. At 16	Child, Youth and Family Services Act, 2017, s. 85(1); Children's Law Reform Act, s. 65

Age at which a minor may leave home	Relevant legal provision(s)
Prince Edward Island. At 16 to 18, depending on the circumstances	Family Law Act, s. 31(2); Child Protection Act, ss. 13(2) and 13(6)
Québec. At 18 or when emancipated	Civil Code, article 602
Saskatchewan. Generally at 16; until 18, may be apprehended if in need of protection	Child and Family Services Act, ss. 2(1)(d), 7(2), and 18
Yukon. At 19	Child and Family Services Act, ss. 1 and 31

If you are under 16, and especially if you are under 14, you need to be aware that a person who helps you leave home—for example, by giving you another place to live—could be in serious trouble. If you leave home when you are under 14 and another person lets you stay with him or her, intending to keep your parents from having you with them, he or she can be charged with abduction under the Criminal Code of Canada (s. 281). This also applies if you are staying with a parent who is keeping you from being with another parent or guardian who has the right to have you with him or her (Criminal Code, ss. 282 and 283). If you are under 16 and unmarried, and someone helps you to leave home by taking you away from your parents against their will, they can be charged with abduction under section 280 of the Criminal Code. (But if you are over 14 and they just let you stay with them, they will not be charged).

Emancipation

Article 602 of the Québec Civil Code explicitly says, "No unemancipated minor may leave his domicile without the consent of the person having parental authority." Emancipation is a legal status, recognized in the province of Québec, that allows a minor to acquire many of the rights of an adult. There are two ways in which you can become emancipated:

- By asking your parents to emancipate you (article 167). When you reach the age of 16, your tutor (a parent or other legal guardian) can submit a "declaration of emancipation" to an official called the "Public Curator." The declaration must include your written consent, the consent of your tutor, and the consent of a "tutorship council," which is usually made up of three people who are from your family or who know your family and who act in an advisory role to your tutor.

- By asking the court yourself (article 168). At any age, you can file a request for emancipation with the Superior Court of Québec. The court will consider your reasons for wanting emancipation, as well as the opinions of your tutor (and of the tutorship council, if one exists). It will also consider whether the emancipation is in your best interests. A court will usually emancipate you only for serious reasons and only once you are well into your teens and seem mature enough to take care of yourself. So, before filing for emancipation, it might be wise to consult with a lawyer about your reasons for doing so and about your chances of succeeding.

Once you are emancipated, you are free from your parents' authority and can establish your own household (Civil Code, article 171). In addition, you no longer have to be represented by your tutor in order to exercise your civil rights and can now perform "all acts of simple administration," such as signing a lease or other contract, in your own name (articles 170 and 172). This is called *simple emancipation*. However, when it comes to legal actions that could have serious consequences, especially for your financial situation—accepting a gift that places you under certain obligations, for example, or borrowing large amounts of money—you still need the help of your tutor or the permission of the court (articles 173 and 174).

If you get married, you are automatically granted *full emancipation*, which allows you to exercise all your civil rights as if you were of full age. But you may also apply to the court for full emancipation, provided you have a very serious reason for making this request. In deciding whether to grant it, the court will again seek the advice of your tutor and of the tutorship council, if there is one (articles 175 and 176). If you are emancipated, you can—and should—ask the clerk of the court to issue you a *certificate of emancipation*, so that you can prove that you are emancipated; the certificate will state whether the emancipation is simple or full (article 176.1).

Discipline

If you disobey your parents, they have a right (though not an obligation) to punish you—within reason. This punishment could take the form of depriving you of something you want, like not letting you go to a party that you were really looking forward to, or it might consist of ordering you to do something that isn't especially fun to do, such as doing extra chores for the next month. (Most parents remember such punishments from when they were growing up.) But are parents allowed to punish their children *physically*? That is, do they have a right to hit you?

Corporal punishment, as it's called, is one of the oldest and most debated ways of disciplining young people. It includes spanking, slapping, and any other punishment that's meant to hurt you or cause you physical discomfort. Ordinarily, hitting someone makes you guilty of "assault," which is a *crime*. Yet, even though assault is against the law, section 43 of the Criminal Code still allows the use of "force" as a way of disciplining a child:

> Every schoolteacher, parent or person standing in the place of a parent is justified in using force by way of correction toward a pupil or child, as the case may be, who is under his care, if the force does not exceed what is reasonable under the circumstances.

In the past, judges trying criminal cases in which a parent or other adult had been accused of assaulting a child held widely differing opinions about what "reasonable force" was. Some parents were convicted for using too much physical force, while others were **acquitted** even after inflicting very serious beatings. Eventually, in a case titled *Canadian Foundation for Children, Youth and the Law v. Canada (Attorney General)* (2004 SCC 4 [CanLII]), the Supreme Court was asked to determine whether section 43 of the Criminal Code violated children's constitutional rights. The majority of the justices refused to declare the law unconstitutional, but they did put important limits on it. In the judgment of the Court, in order for corporal punishment to be "reasonable," it must follow these rules:

- Only parents and guardians may use it, not teachers or temporary caregivers.

- Corporal punishment can be legally used only on children aged 2 to 12, when the young person can (supposedly) learn from it.

- The force used must be light and must not cause major or long-lasting pain or harm. It must not be inflicted in a degrading or inhuman way.

- It must not be inflicted with an object (such as a wooden spoon, belt, strap, or cane).

- It must not include "blows or slaps to the head." (This is generally taken to mean that parents may not slap your face, although it's not completely clear whether, by "head," the court meant anywhere from the neck up or just the top of the head—the cranium.)

- Its purpose should be to improve behaviour; parents should not spank simply because they are angry, frustrated, or simply abusive.

So, provided it follows these rules, spanking a child is considered legal. Otherwise, it is criminal assault and can be prosecuted.

In 1994, when Québec revised its Civil Code, it eliminated an article that allowed parents to use "reasonable and moderate" punishment on their children. Today, many people in Canada (including the Truth and Reconciliation Commission) feel that section 43 of the Criminal Code should be repealed. In fact, Bill S-206, which is currently in the Senate, would do just that. Physical punishment allows parents to hurt a child in a way that they cannot hurt another adult, and many experts question whether such punishment is actually effective (or whether punishment of *any* sort is a good way to teach children how to behave). In 2006, the United Nations Committee on the Rights of the Child issued a statement that aimed to underscore "the obligation of all States parties to move quickly to prohibit and eliminate all corporal punishment," as such punishment violates several articles of the Convention on the Rights of the Child.[10] Many

10 This is from the UN committee's "General Comment No. 8 (2006): The Right of the Child to Protection from Corporal Punishment and Other Cruel or Degrading Forms of Punishment," https:// resourcecentre.savethechildren.net/sites/default/files/documents/ gc8.pdf, para. 2. In particular, article 19, paragraph (1), of the Convention instructs governments to "take all appropriate legislative, administrative, social and educational measures to protect the child

countries now forbid spanking, as well as other physically and emotionally harmful forms of discipline. If section 43 is repealed, as we hope it will be, Canada will join the growing list of places that have given young people the same protection against violence that adults have.

Divorce

Some marriages end with the couple deciding to go their separate ways, and some couples who divorce have children. In addition to the federal Divorce Act, several provincial family laws deal with divorce. To get divorced, a couple has to go to court to have a judge end the marriage, to divide their property between them, and to decide what part each parent will play in their children's lives. Some divorce cases are very simple because the couple has already considered these issues and come to an agreement. But when two people each want something different, and neither one is willing to let go beyond a certain point, divorce can be a slow and very difficult process.

When parents divorce, two big decisions must be made about their children. The first concerns **custody**. Which parent will the children live with—and who will have the right to make major decisions about them? There are several possible arrangements:

---

from all forms of physical or mental violence, injury or abuse, neglect or negligent treatment, maltreatment or exploitation, including sexual abuse, while in the care of parent(s), legal guardian(s) or any other person who has the care of the child."

- *sole custody,* where the children live with only one parent and that parent has the main responsibility for them.

- *joint custody,* where both parents share responsibility for the children. In some cases, the children will spend more or less equal time with both parents (this is also called *shared custody*); in other cases, they will live mainly with one parent, but the other parent will still be equally responsible for their care and for making decisions about them.

- *split custody,* a less common arrangement where one parent has custody of one or more of the children and the other has custody of the other(s).

Custody arrangements lead to the second big decision. Especially in cases of sole custody, the judge must decide how much **access** to give the other parent. Access means the right to see and spend time with the children, as well as the right to be given important information about them by the other parent. Access arrangements differ from one case to another. Sometimes children spend a lot of time with both parents; sometimes they see one parent only on certain weekends. There are even cases—although these are extremely rare—where a judge has ordered parents to take turns living with their children in the same house.

Some lawmakers argue that talking in terms of "custody" and "access" places too much emphasis on children as some sort of object and encourages parents to focus on their rights over their children rather than on their parental obligations. So, in place of these terms, some provincial laws now adopt expressions such as "parental responsibilities" and "parenting time" and, more generally, try to ensure that both parents will continue to play an active part in their children's lives in the event of separation or divorce.

 Do I have any say about which parent I will live with?

The final decision on this one belongs to your parents and the court—but you may be able to state your opinion and have some influence on what happens to you. If your parents have already agreed on who will have custody of you, the judge will normally respect their decision. If they don't agree, the judge will make the decision, and, according to the federal Divorce Act, this decision must be made in your best interests. In this case, you may have a say. The laws of some provinces require—or at least encourage—judges to take into account the children's wishes when making decisions about custody and access. Some judges will even talk directly with children about this, but more often the judge will have another adult speak to the children and then report their wishes to the court. One way or another, according to article 12 of the Convention on the Rights of the Child, you should be given an opportunity to be heard.

The chances that your wishes will be taken seriously are greater in the following circumstances:

- The judge is convinced that you are really sure of what you want.

- The judge believes that your choice is really your own and that you haven't been influenced by your parents. For example, it won't look good if the parent you choose happens to have been buying you lots of presents.

- You seem to have thought about which of your parents is likely to take better care of you.

- You are a teenager. Not only does it make sense that an older child will know better what he or she wants, but judges are often reluctant to make decisions that go against the wishes of teenagers, who might be more likely to run away or otherwise refuse to respect a custody order and who are getting close to the age when they can leave home anyway.

If your parents are fighting for custody of you, and no one seems interested in your own wishes, you might try to get help from a social worker or even a lawyer (see the list of resources in appendix C). Such a person may be willing to bring your views before the court and at least make sure they are heard.

Once the judgment is made, you have to live with the parent who gets custody of you. However, that parent must cooperate with access orders and not do anything to stop the other parent from seeing you during access time. In fact, as we saw above, in connection with abduction, there are laws against withholding access to a child.[11] A parent might be

---

11 Provinces also have laws about withholding access. For example, in Ontario, if a parent refuses to allow a child to visit the other parent, section 36 of the Children's Law Reform Act makes it possible for the parent who has been granted access to obtain a court order directing the police "to locate, apprehend and deliver the child to the person named in the order."

able to go to court in the future and ask for a new custody or access order; however, there would probably have to be strong reasons for changing the original arrangement.

When you reach the age at which you can leave home in your province, you can generally move in with the parent who does not have custody of you if that is your preference. However, in some provinces, parents may request to have a custody order enforced until you reach the age of majority, even if you can legally leave home at an earlier age. In a recent Ontario court case, for example, *L. (N.) v. M. (R.R.)* (2016 ONSC 809 [CanLII]), two brothers were caught in the middle of a bitter custody battle between their parents, in which they firmly sided with their mother. The original custody order, issued when the younger son was not quite 16 and the older one well over 17, gave full custody to their father—much against the sons' wishes. Their mother filed a motion to have the order changed so that she would have custody, and, in response, the father filed a motion to have the original order enforced. The sons asked instead that *no* custody order be made, declaring that they had withdrawn from parental control, as allowed by section 65 of the Children's Law Reform Act. In the end, the judge cancelled the original custody order (including a condition that allowed the police to enforce it) and ruled that "no person has custody or access rights over either of the sons" (para. 150).

FACT FILE   **The Case of Clayton Giles**

The story of Clayton Giles of Alberta is a good example both of the challenges that a child of divorce can face and the influence that a young person can have if he or she is persistent. When Clayton was 4, his parents divorced. His mother would not accept sharing custody with his father and ended up winning sole custody. Clayton was unhappy with this situation as he had a better relationship with his father than with his mother and would have wanted to have equal time with both of them. But his mother's efforts to keep him away from his father were so persistent that, at one point, he did not see him for three years. Eventually, Clayton had enough of it. When he was 13, he ran away to his father several times. On his second attempt, the police were called. They asked him whom he wanted to be with, and when he said he would prefer to stay with his father, they left him alone.

Clayton then decided to become politically active and protest the injustice he saw in judges not giving enough consideration to the views of children of divorcing parents. In 2001, when he was 14, he held a nineteen-day hunger strike in front of a Calgary courtroom, and he also set up a website to promote his cause. Soon after, a judge granted sole custody to his father. Even though his own battle had been won, Clayton then travelled on foot and by bicycle across Canada and the United States, collecting signatures for a petition to give more of a voice to children whose parents divorce—another battle, one that is still going on.

Courts generally want to see both parents involved in their children's lives. Sometimes, though, a divorcing parent will try to turn children against the other parent. That is, the parent will try to *alienate* the children from the other parent. For example, one parent might repeatedly criticize the other parent or tell the children stories about that parent that may not be entirely true—to the point that the children come to dislike that parent. A parent may also try to win the children over by buying them a lot of presents or being unusually kind to them. The "alienating" parent may get very angry or even abusive if the children want to see the other parent or otherwise display affection for him or her. Such a parent might also try to stop the other parent from having access to the children, despite what the court ordered.

How courts deal with such a parent will vary from case to case, but if the judge thinks that one parent is not being honest about the other parent, the judge may order mediation. In this case, a mediator—a professional trained to help people resolve differences—will work with the family to try to mend relationships and establish some sort of peace. Sometimes the judge may take more decisive steps. There have been cases where a judge granted custody or access to the parent who had been alienated, even when the child was stubbornly against it. This is indeed what had happened in the Ontario case we just described: the boys' mother had succeeded in alienating them from their father, and, by originally giving him custody, the court was hoping to undo the damage (although this effort obviously failed). In one case—*Bruni v. Bruni* (2010 ONSC 6568 [CanLII])—a judge decided to punish a mother who had effectively destroyed the relationship between her estranged husband and their daughter by reducing the spousal support payments he owed her to one dollar a month. The judge also found that the mother had so thoroughly alienated the daughter from her father that enforcing access would not be in the daughter's best interests.

Youth and families who are in such painful situations would do well to get counselling in order to try to sort things out. Depending on the circumstances, it could also be advisable to find a lawyer to represent a child's interests. In Ontario, the Office of the Children's Lawyer might agree to take the case for free.[12]

As this chapter illustrates, the law still gives parents extensive power over the lives of their children. Of course, parents also have legal responsibilities toward their children, but these duties are described in fairly broad terms and may be difficult to enforce at times. This raises the question of whether our laws should be changed to make it clearer that parental authority is not absolute and that youth have the right to make some of their own decisions, especially as they get older. We believe that you are your own person and that it's not fair for parents to expect blind obedience from you. As we saw, Alberta's Family Law Act already requires parents to exercise their powers

---

12 Either the parents or their child can contact the Office of the Children's Lawyer, but it exists to represent the interests of the child, not the parents. However, representing someone's interests—that is, making sure the person's views get a fair hearing—isn't necessarily the same thing as agreeing with those views.

"in a manner consistent with the evolving capacity of the child." So does the Convention on the Rights of the Child. Perhaps it's time for the rest of Canada to do likewise. At a bare minimum, laws throughout Canada could be changed to incorporate the principle that parental authority dwindles as a child becomes more mature. Doing so would give young people the legal right to exercise at least some degree of influence over decisions that affect them.

But, as we see it, there is a deeper issue here. As we mentioned earlier, in our society the relationship between a parent and a child is considered to be a private matter, in which the law has no business interfering, except in cases of serious abuse or neglect. In other words, the law treats the parent-child relationship much like any other personal relationship between two human beings. And yet there is an important difference. People generally choose their friends and their marriage partners—but children do not choose their parents. Instead, when a man and woman have a child, the assumption is that the child "belongs" to the parents, who are automatically entitled to raise the child in whatever way they please (as long as they do not fail to provide the child with the "necessaries of life"). It is therefore up to them to decide how much kindness and attention to give their children, as well as what values to instill in them. Aside from the principle that parents should strive to make decisions in their child's best interests, parents are not expected to answer to any specific standards. Raising a child is not understood to be a job, which parents can perform well or badly. Within certain broad limits, parents are free to come up with their own definition of what raising a child should look like.

Suppose that, instead of viewing child rearing as a personal entitlement and allowing parents more or less free rein in how to do it, the law took a different approach. What if the law laid down some ideal standards for parental behaviour, on the understanding that it is the duty of parents to raise healthy, happy, well-balanced children who will grow up to be responsible and considerate adults? Many people would probably argue that parents have a "right" to decide how to raise their children and that setting out standards would be too "controlling." But the law already sets certain standards of behaviour that people must meet. Quite apart from laws about crimes, people who are doing a job are routinely expected to turn in a satisfactory performance. Others might argue that enforcing such laws would be impossible. Yet they would be no more unenforceable than many other laws on the books. For the most part, laws are enforced not because the police watch over everybody, in hopes of catching someone in the act of committing an offence, but because a person whose rights have been violated files a complaint.

In short, as it presently stands, the law in Canada goes a long way toward letting parents off the hook. Parents are given the lion's share of the rights and liberties, and the law generally leaves them alone unless they do something truly awful. What if we shifted the focus to the rights and liberties of children? What if parents were held accountable for how well they do their job?

GOING TO SCHOOL

By the time you're grown up, you will have spent many hours of your life at school. When we're young, we generally think of going to school as something we *have* to do—which makes sense, because we have little choice but to attend school. But, while we don't usually think of it this way, education is also a right. In fact, article 28 of the Convention on the Rights of the Child obliges governments to "recognize the right of the child to education." So why is education considered a right?

The simplest answer is that education is essential to human development. Without at least some education, we would lack the knowledge and skills we need to take part in adult life. By "skills," we don't just mean "how-to" skills, like learning to use a computer or how to write a grammatically correct sentence. Education helps us learn how to think about things and solve problems, and it also teaches us how to be part of the culture in which we live. We learn these things from other people as well, including our parents and friends, but what they know is only part of the whole picture. So education is designed to ensure that everyone—no matter what their individual circumstances may be—has access to certain basic knowledge and training. Since we deserve to develop into capable adults, education has come to be considered a right.

People differ quite a bit, however, when it comes to how much value they place on education. Some parents, for example, think education is extremely important and want their children to have lots of it; others put more emphasis on education as a way to learn practical skills that will help their children to get jobs. In the past, whether you got an education at all depended a great deal on your family's social position. If you were lucky enough to come from a wealthy family, you could expect to receive an education from in-home tutors or at a private school. If you came from a working-class family, or if you grew up on a farm, you might be sent to school for only a few years, until you were old enough to work. In other words, access to education was very uneven, and to some degree it still is. But this is why we now have compulsory public education—so that you can get a basic education regardless of how much money your family has or whether your parents happen to think that going to school is important.

In Canada, education is mainly under the control of individual provinces and territories, whose governments spend substantial sums of public money on their school systems. Partly for that reason, and partly just because educating people is an important responsibility, the law takes a big interest in the education you receive. In looking at what the law has to say on the subject, we'll use Ontario as our main source of legal examples, although we'll also point out general principles that apply in every province and territory.

The Right—and the Duty—to Attend School

In Canada (as in many other countries), everyone has the right to free public schooling. For example, section 32(1) of Ontario's Education Act states: "A person has the right, without payment of a fee, to attend a school in a school section, separate school zone or secondary school district, as the case may be, in which the person is qualified to be a resident pupil." This is followed by several sections that explain in detail how a "resident pupil" is defined—but the point is that you're expected to attend a school in the school district where you and your parents live. This is generally the case in Canada, although in some places (such as Alberta) or in special circumstances, you may be allowed to attend a school somewhere else.

Your right to free public schooling lasts until you finish high school: it doesn't necessarily end when you reach a certain age. In Ontario, for example, there's no limit on the number of years you can spend in high school (although there is an upper limit to the number of course credits you can earn). Moreover, even though most people complete middle school around the age of 13 or 14, you have the legal right in Ontario to attend elementary (primary and middle) school until you turn 21—and if your birthday falls before the last day of school in June, you have the right to stay in school until the end of the school year. Once you graduate from high school, though, you're not entitled to free post-secondary education. Universities and colleges are restrictive, in the sense that they can choose whom to admit—and, even though, in Canada, most universities and colleges are public institutions (that is, they are funded partly by the government), they generally require students to pay tuition.[1]

Although you have a right to education, you are not given a choice about whether to exercise this right. No matter where in the country you live, education is *compulsory* up to a certain age. As a general rule, compulsory education begins in the year that a child turns 6. In most of Canada, you must stay in school until you turn 16 (unless you manage to graduate from high school earlier); the exceptions are Manitoba, New Brunswick, and Ontario, where the school-leaving age has been raised to 18. There can be consequences for both you and your parents if you don't go to school—although, of course, you can miss specific days if there's a good reason, such as illness. According to section 30(1) of Ontario's Education Act, for instance, your parents or guardians face a fine of up to $200 if they fail to make sure you're at school, at least until you turn 16. And, according to section 30(5), a student who is at least 12 and

---

1 An exception is the system of junior colleges (CEGEPs) in Québec, which is relatively well funded by the province. CEGEPs are either free or else charge much lower tuition fees than universities.

under 16 and who regularly refuses to attend school commits an offence and is liable either to be fined or to be put under **probation** (in which case the student must abide by the rules of the probation order). "Why only until the age of 16, if the school-leaving age is 18?" You may be asking at this point. The answer lies in a slight quirk in the law. When the school-leaving age was raised to 18 in Ontario, the intention was to provide for similar penalties pertaining to students who have turned 16 but are not yet 18. However, these penalties have yet to be incorporated into the Education Act—so, as matters presently stand, the courts have little ability to enforce the law that students must remain in school until they turn 18.

Even when you do reach the school-leaving age, you may not be able to drop out right on your birthday: you may have to wait for the end of the school year. To use our example of Ontario again: section 21(1)(b) of the Education Act says that you must remain in school until the last school day in June in the year in which you turn 18. But this also means that you can leave school before you actually turn 18 if your birthday happens to fall after the last school day in June in that year.

Education Options

Even though education itself is compulsory, not all schools are public schools—that is, schools that are paid for by the government. Other options do exist:

- **Private schools**: These are run by private citizens
  outside the public education system, and your parents must pay to enrol you in such a school. Each
  school makes its own rules about who can attend, and
  private schools often have other special rules—for
  example, about school hours or whether students
  must wear a school uniform. The school curriculum
  may also differ a little from the standard public school
  curriculum. However, private schools must operate
  within certain rules set by law, and their teaching
  must meet standards set by the province.

- **Religion-based schools**: These are schools that are
  affiliated with a particular religion. These schools
  exist for people who believe that education should
  include religious or spiritual instruction. In addition
  to various Christian schools, there are, for example,
  Jewish, Muslim, Buddhist, and Sikh schools. For the
  most part, these schools are private, and whether
  they receive any funding from the government
  depends on the province in which they are located.
  However, Alberta, Ontario, and Saskatchewan, as well
  as Yellowknife, in the Northwest Territories, have
  separate Catholic or Protestant schools that are part
  of the public system, and you can attend them for
  free, even if your family isn't Catholic or Protestant.

- **Homeschooling**: All provinces and territories allow
  parents to educate their children at home themselves
  instead of sending them to school, but the rules for
  doing so differ from place to place. In Nova Scotia, for
  instance, parents who wish to educate their children

at home have to register with the Department of Education and Early Childhood Development; in Newfoundland and Labrador, they need to get permission from the school district. In order to receive a high school diploma, however, a homeschooled child must take GED (General Educational Development) exams—that is, high school equivalency exams.

There are also different options within the public system, depending on what part of Canada and what school district you live in. For example, there are alternative schools for young people who want to focus on special talents; at the secondary school level, there are traditional high schools, some technical and trade schools, and other schools with apprenticeship programs. Some high schools offer co-op programs that make it possible for students to work part-time to earn credits toward their diploma while at the same time gaining valuable work experience. Also, by the time you reach the secondary level, not all subjects are compulsory. A typical Canadian high school offers a range of elective subjects, so you can, to some extent, choose your own study program. This is especially true in big cities, which generally have more schools and programs available than a small community can offer.

 Do I have any control over the education I get?

If you have all these choices, can you make any of them yourself? The written law of many provinces doesn't clearly answer the question of whether children or parents have the power to make these choices. Usually, though, the people who run schools tend to assume that parents have the power to make decisions for their minor children.[2] Normally, then, you need a parent or guardian to enrol you in school. As long as your parents respect the laws on compulsory education, they can decide which school to enrol you in, and they can also take you out of the school you are enrolled in.[3] (In fact, in Québec, sections 4 and 239 of the Education Act specifically say that until you are 18, your parents have the right to choose your school from the ones available in your school district). Even on the relatively minor and very personal question of which elective subjects to take, your school will likely want your parents to approve your choices unless you are an adult student.[4] This is *general* information; we can't tell you exactly what a given school would do if a minor student, especially one in high school, wanted to

---

2 However, a court can overrule parents' educational preferences if it finds that those preferences do not serve the child's best interests. For example, in *Eaton v. Brant County Board of Education* (1997 CanLII 366 [SCC]), the Supreme Court ruled that a girl with cerebral palsy would do better if she were placed in a special education class, even though her parents wanted her to stay in a regular classroom.

3 If you are staying temporarily with an adult who is not your legal guardian, some schools will allow that person to enrol you in school and approve your education choices, in place of your parents.

4 Sometimes parents want to pull their children out of classes because they don't approve of the curriculum. Some of these cases have ended up in court. For example, in a 2012 case (*S.L. v. Commission scolaire des Chênes*, 2012 SCC 7 [CanLII]), a group of parents tried to get the Supreme Court of Canada to rule that not being able to take their children out of a class that taught about different religions went against their freedom of religion. The Supreme Court disagreed and did not allow them to take their children out of class.

make a choice that differed from his or her parents' choice. Some schools in some places *might* allow minor students the power to make their own, independent choices about which school to attend or which subjects to take (and you can always check this with your school or school board), but many schools will not.

However, there is at least one situation in which you should be able to take control of your own educational choices. As we explained in chapter 3, in most provinces, you can withdraw from your parents' control once you reach the age of 16 and establish your independence, or under some circumstances, live with someone other than your parents. In this case, even though you are still a minor, you may qualify as an "independent student." For example, Alberta defines an independent student as one who is either 18 or older (that is, legally an adult) or else 16 or older and living independently. Such a student is entitled to the same rights and benefits and is subject to the same obligations as his or her parents, "and the student's parent shall not exercise those rights, receive those benefits or be subject to those obligations" (School Act, ss. 1[1] and 1[3]). Similarly, in New Brunswick, an "independent pupil" is one who has reached the age of 19 (the age of majority in that province) or is living independently of his or her parents (Education Act, s. 1).

If you are no longer under parental control, you should be able to enrol in school, stay enrolled, and choose the subjects you will study without having to get your parents' approval. If you withdraw from parental control while you are still in school, *you should immediately go to your principal and let him or her know that you have done so*. You should explain that you intend to make your own decisions about your schooling and ask the school not to let your parents do so in your place. Not all schools will be familiar with the idea of withdrawing from parental control. If a school refuses to enrol you or otherwise allow you to make decisions about your education, even though you have legally left home, *you should get a lawyer to help you*. You may need to write your principal a letter stating your intention to be an independent student.[5]

If you and your parents disagree about education choices, it can help to go to your school's principal or guidance counsellor, who may be willing to talk with your parents. By the time you reach high school, your school principal and guidance counsellor are more likely to be willing to try to intercede in such conflicts. Especially in cases where they feel that your preference was based on good reasons and/ or that your parents are behaving in an arbitrary fashion. You might also be able to find support in the form of mediation services, services that are available in some provinces through the education system.

As a general rule, your parents are entitled to view the records your school keeps about you. In Ontario, both you and your parents have the right to examine your student records; after you turn 18, only you have the right to do so

---

5 You can find a sample of such a letter on the Legal Rights Wiki of Justice for Children and Youth: http://jfcy.org/en/rights/ leaving-home-rights/. (Scroll down to "Sample Letter—School.")

(Education Act, s. 266[3]). In some situations, the school might wish to share information with your parents (for example, about a suspension), but if you are over 16 and have withdrawn from parental control, you may be able to prevent the school from doing so.

Depending on where you live, you might have an opportunity to influence decisions about school policy. In a number of provinces, school boards are allowed to have "student trustees"—students who attend meetings of the board to represent the interests of students. They can take part in discussions and give voice to student wishes and concerns, although they generally don't have the same status as regular members of the board. In Ontario, for example, a student trustee can suggest a motion but not actually move one; neither can a student trustee vote on a motion, although he or she can require that the board vote on a matter under discussion (Education Act, s. 55). In Québec, Secondary Cycle Two schools (grades 9 through 11) are required to allow students to form a student committee that collaborates in developing and implementing the school's educational program and can also make suggestions about how the school operates. In addition, these committees appoint student representatives to sit on the school's governing board—or, if no such committee or student association exists, then the principal must arrange for the election of student representatives (Québec Education Act, ss. 96.5, 96.6, and s. 51). This system has the advantage of giving students a voice at the level of individual schools.

School Rules

Any school will have a set of rules that students must follow. These rules will differ in their details, which will largely depend on what makes sense to the adults who run your local schools. Provincial or territorial education laws may also provide some guidance to schools about how to set rules. In Ontario, for instance, there is a province-wide code of conduct for schools, authorized by section 301(1) of the Education Act. In addition, according to sections 302(1) and 302(2), every school board is responsible for setting a code of conduct for its schools, as well as its own rules for disciplining students.

 Can the school impose a dress code or uniform?

Rules about students' appearance exist in many schools. Ontario's Education Act authorizes the Minister of Education to require a public school board to make rules about "appropriate dress" for students (s. 302[5]). The dress codes of many schools don't limit you all that much, but many private schools, all of Ontario's separate schools, and a few public schools have chosen to make their students wear uniforms. Adults will give you all sorts of reasons why they think it's a good idea to deny you the freedom to choose your own clothes in the morning, despite the fact that millions of people have managed to get a good education while attending schools that didn't tell them what to wear. It could be argued that school uniforms, at least in the public system, go against your Charter right to freedom of expression, guaranteed in section 2(b); however, a Canadian court has yet to decide on the issue in this way.

One thing that the law is clear on, however, is that dress codes must not violate your freedom of religion, as guaranteed in section 2(a) of the Charter of Rights and Freedoms. Courts have ruled that students are entitled to wear items of religious dress, such as Jewish yarmulkes, Muslim hijabs, or Sikh turbans. Even the right to wear the Sikh curved dagger, or kirpan—which technically qualifies as bringing a weapon to school—was upheld by the Supreme Court of Canada in *Multani v. Commission scolaire Marguerite-Bourgeoys* (2006 SCC 6 [CanLII]), although the case suggests that the school may impose reasonable safety rules on the wearer.

 Can the school open my locker?

Yes, if the school has a good reason to believe that you may be hiding something illegal or dangerous. Ordinarily, as we will explain in chapter 8, the police cannot conduct a search without a **warrant**—that is, without written permission from a judge. But schools are an exception. The 1998 Supreme Court case *R. v. M. (M.R.)* (1998 CanLII 770 [SCC]) dealt with the issue of student searches. Two junior high school students were called to the vice-principal's office after another student reported that they were planning to sell drugs at a school dance. The vice-principal, who had made sure that a police officer was present, said he was going to search them. In the course of the search, one of the students was found to have a bag of marijuana hidden in one of his socks. The officer arrested him and then, in the company of the student, went on to inspect his locker, where no more drugs were found. The student sued, and the case went all the way to the Supreme Court. The student's legal counsel argued that because section 8 of the Charter of Rights and Freedoms protects people against "unreasonable search or seizure," the student's rights had been violated. But the court ruled that the search was actually *not* unreasonable. As the court saw it, the government has a duty to keep schools safe, and so someone who is on school property cannot reasonably expect to have the same degree of privacy there as elsewhere. The court also found that the way the search was conducted was in line with the rules for doing so.

However, in this and other cases, the courts have also ruled that schools should have good reason for limiting students' privacy. If the school suspects that a student is hiding drugs or weapons, this qualifies as a good reason for a search. But if the school thinks that the student is hiding chewing gum, a toy, or some other harmless object that he or she is not supposed to bring to school, this may not be a good reason. Also, to search a student's *person*, the school needs a stronger reason than it does to search a student's locker or desk, and personal searches must be handled very carefully and respectfully. This is because your clothes—and your body—are private: they belong to you, while your locker belongs to the school and is just on loan to you during the school year.

LGBTQA Rights in School

In 2012, the Ontario legislature passed Bill 13, the "Accepting Schools Act." This law amended the Education Act to require publicly funded schools to create a safe and supportive environment for gay, bisexual, and transgender students. If you are an LGBTQA student or a friend of such a student, your school must not discriminate against you, and this is true whether you attend a standard public school or a separate (Catholic) school. In practice, this law means, for instance, that your school cannot stop you from founding a "Gay-Straight Alliance" or similar club. It also means that the school should respect the name you go by to express your gender and your choice of pronoun (whether *he*, *she*, *they*, or something else). In addition, you have the right to go to a prom with a same-sex date and, if there is a school uniform, to use the one that reflects your chosen gender.

The courts have found that section 15 of the Charter of Rights protects you from discrimination on the basis of your sexual orientation. Various federal, provincial, and territorial human rights codes also require government agencies to respect the rights of gay and transgender people. Therefore, schools and boards of education are slowly changing their policies with regard to issues such as whether to designate gender-neutral washrooms or whether to allow transgender students to join either a male or a female sports team, as they prefer. Student privacy is another very important aspect of LGBTQA rights. For example, Alberta recently amended the School Act to say that schools are not to let parents know that their child has joined a gay-straight alliance club. The Vancouver School Board made "confidentiality"—respecting the privacy of gay and transgender students—part of its rules on LGBTQA students in 2014. Nevertheless, not only are LGBTQA rights an area in which the law is still developing, but society can be slow to catch up with the law. So it's wise to check your local school board's policy on matters pertaining to sexual orientation and choice of gender.

Consequences for Breaking the Rules

As a general rule, teachers are allowed to discipline students within reason, and their discipline should be similar to that of a kind, firm, and judicious parent. Whatever methods they choose, though, corporal punishment is no longer allowed in school. Teachers may use physical force only for restraining students when they need to physically control them; they may not hit or hurt them as punishment. The Supreme Court of Canada decided this in *Canadian Foundation for Children, Youth and the Law v. Canada* (2004 SCC 4 [CanLII]), which we discussed in chapter 3. The vast majority of provinces and territories have additionally banned corporal punishment in their own laws about public schools.

For some offences, you can be suspended (temporarily forbidden to enter the school) or, for more serious offences, expelled (kept out for an indefinite period of time or even permanently). In Ontario, the reasons for which a principal must *consider* suspending you are found in section 306(1) of the Education Act:

1. Uttering a threat to inflict serious bodily harm on another person.

2. Possessing alcohol or illegal drugs or, unless the pupil is a medical cannabis user, cannabis.

3. Being under the influence of alcohol or, unless the pupil is a medical cannabis user, cannabis.

4. Swearing at a teacher or at another person in a position of authority.

5. Committing an act of vandalism that causes extensive damage to school property at the pupil's school or to property located on the premises of the pupil's school.

6. Bullying.

7. Any other activity that is an activity for which a principal may suspend a pupil under a policy of the board.

Even if you didn't do one of these things during school hours or on school property (for example, if you bullied a classmate over the weekend), you may still be suspended if what you did could affect the overall atmosphere at the school.

According to section 306(4) of the Education Act, you may be suspended for one to twenty school days. During this period, you cannot attend classes, but, depending on the duration of the suspension, you will either be given a homework package or offered a program for suspended students. As section 308 specifies, the principal must let your teachers know about the suspension, and you must be given written notice of it—and, unless you are 18 or are 16 or 17 and have withdrawn from parental control, your parents must receive written notice as well.

Because a suspension goes on your school record and can work to your disadvantage later on, you may wish to appeal a suspension to the district school board (or other such authority)—although, according to the rules laid out in section 309 of the act, unless you are 18 or are 16 or 17 and have withdrawn from parental control, your parents will have to make the appeal on your behalf. Notice of the intention to appeal must be received by the board within ten school days from the beginning of the suspension, and the board must hear and decide the appeal within fifteen school days of receiving the notice. The hearing will be similar to a trial, in that both sides will have a chance to defend their position. Even if your parents made the appeal, you are allowed to be present at the hearing and make your own statement; it is also possible to have a lawyer represent you. If the board decides that the suspension was not imposed fairly, the suspension will end (if it hasn't already) and will be erased from your school record.

For some quite serious offences, the principal *must* suspend you. According to section 310(1) of the Ontario Education Act, these offences are:

1. Possessing a weapon, including possessing a firearm.

2. Using a weapon to cause or to threaten bodily harm to another person.

3. Committing physical assault on another person that causes bodily harm requiring treatment by a medical practitioner.

4. Committing sexual assault.

5. Trafficking in weapons or in illegal drugs.

6. Committing robbery.

7. Giving alcohol or cannabis to a minor.

7.1. Bullying, if,

> i. the pupil has previously been suspended for engaging in bullying, and

> ii. the pupil's continuing presence in the school creates an unacceptable risk to the safety of another person.

7.2. Any activity listed in subsection 306(1) that is motivated by bias, prejudice or hate based on race, national or ethnic origin, language, colour, religion, sex, age, mental or physical disability, sexual orientation, gender identity, gender expression, or any other similar factor.

8. Any other activity that, under a policy of a board, is an activity for which a principal must suspend a pupil and, therefore in accordance with this Part,

conduct an investigation to determine whether to recommend to the board that the pupil be expelled.

In the case of such offences, the written notice of the suspension must include information about the investigation that the principal will carry out before deciding whether to recommend expulsion. Section 311.1 contains rules about how this investigation will proceed. If the principal recommends the expulsion, the board will hold a hearing, again similar to a trial at which the voices of all sides are heard (see s. 311.3).

If the board decides to expel you, it will choose either to exclude you only from your school or to exclude you from all the schools in the board's district. In the first case, the board will assign you to a new school within its district; in the second, it will assign you to a program for expelled students (Education Act, s. 311.5). You can apply to enrol at a school in another board's district, but you might not be admitted unless you move to that district—and, in any case, the new school will learn about your expulsion when it gets your record, which could affect how the school treats you.

An expulsion is not necessarily permanent: the Education Act (s. 311.7) makes it possible to appeal an expulsion to a special tribunal, and you can ask to return to school if you successfully complete a program for expelled students. Still, you will lose a lot of time in this way, and it can seriously affect your education. All in all, then, it's better not to get yourself expelled in the first place.

Bullying

Bullying is an issue that schools are now taking very seriously. In Ontario, for example, bullying is defined in detail in section 1(1) of the Education Act as any "aggressive and typically repeated" behaviour by a pupil that can cause harm, fear, or distress to someone else or create a negative school environment for that person. This behaviour can include not only physical violence or threats of violence but also any other kind of intimidation. *Intimidation* means anything that gives or seems to give the bully more power over the bullied person because of differences between them in size, strength, age, intelligence, peer group power, economic or social status, family circumstances, religion, race or ethnic origin, sexual orientation, gender, gender identity or expression, disability, or the need to receive special education. Bullying is not necessarily physical. It includes things that the bully says to or about the person being bullied or writes about them. *Cyberbullying* (also called online harassment) refers to using the Internet to engage in bullying behaviour; this includes repeatedly sending insulting or intimidating messages to someone via text messaging or email, as well as spreading negative or embarrassing information about someone via social networking sites and services such as Facebook or Twitter. Cyberbullying is an especially cowardly form of bullying, since it allows a bully to avoid having to actually confront another person.

In recent years, quite a few provinces have passed laws that define bullying and require schools to deal with it.

In Ontario, the Education Act expects school boards to prevent bullying, to regularly educate teachers and other staff about preventing bullying and about how to foster a positive atmosphere at school, and to have programs that deal with bullies and help students who have been bullied. In Ontario schools, the week beginning on the third Sunday in each November is now "Bullying Awareness and Prevention Week."

Many things that bullies do are not merely cruel but are in fact *crimes* and may be prosecuted as such. Such crimes include physically attacking a victim, threatening him or her, encouraging him or her to commit suicide, sending false or harassing messages or making similar phone calls, or threatening someone in order to get money from him or her. Bullying behaviour that causes the victim to fear for his or her own safety or for the safety of someone the victim knows constitutes "criminal harassment," as defined in section 264 of the Criminal Code.

As the law recognizes, no one should have to live with bullying. If you experience it, you should immediately report it to your school. If the school is unhelpful, you and your parents should consider talking to a lawyer and, if the bullying includes possible criminal activity, involving the police. Under no circumstances should you blame yourself for the bullying or feel that you somehow deserve it. You don't.

Disciplining the Teacher

As with students, teachers may not behave any way they want to at school. While doing their work, teachers must meet certain standards and should not be disrespectful or abusive toward students. Otherwise, there may be legal consequences. In Ontario, any member of the public—including a student or his or her parents—may file a complaint against a teacher with the Ontario College of Teachers (OCT), the office that licenses teachers. In order for the OCT to consider the complaint, it must be related to professional misconduct, incompetence, or incapacity on the part of the teacher, it must not be frivolous or made for an improper purpose (such as retaliation), and there shouldn't be any other good reason not to investigate the complaint (Ontario College of Teachers Act, 1996, s. 26[2]). If there is a hearing and the complaint proves to be justified, the teacher will be subject to some sort of penalty, which, depending on how serious the offence was, may range from a reprimand to losing his or her licence to teach.

Filing a complaint is a serious matter. If a teacher behaves in a way that is thoroughly inappropriate and/or unprofessional (to say nothing of out-and-out illegal), then this behaviour should be brought to the attention of the authorities, especially if the behaviour could affect other students. But people who file complaints over relatively minor offences are sometimes seen as troublemakers, and doing so could result in bad relations with your school. So if you have a complaint about a teacher, it is generally best to talk with the principal of your school before going all the way up to the OCT, in hopes that the situation can be resolved in some other way.

Religion in School

In the United States, it has long been considered unacceptable to teach or promote religion in public schools—for example, by expecting students to recite the Lord's Prayer. The First Amendment to the US Constitution guarantees the right to freedom of religion and establishes a principle known as the separation of church and state. So any government institution, including a school, must treat everyone the same, no matter what they believe or don't believe, and should not impose any specific religion. In Canada, this rule is still not fully respected everywhere. This is mainly because, in colonial Canada, Protestant and Catholic schools had certain rights under provincial law, and, at Confederation, these rights were confirmed by section 93 of the 1867 Constitution Act. In 1982, section 29 of the Charter of Rights and Freedoms reconfirmed these rights. So the continued existence of separate religious schools as part of the publicly funded school system is a constitutional right. Today, after some amendments, the Constitution protects separate Protestant or Catholic schools in Alberta, Ontario, and Saskatchewan, and the law also allows them in the three territories. The United Nations has criticized Canada for continuing to fund religious schools with tax money, but this system still exists.

Even in public schools that are not associated with a particular denomination, the law may still allow religious instruction or including prayer in school activities, although this has become less common. In the diverse and multicultural Canada of today, public schools tend to understand that students have different religions or no religion at all and that imposing religion could be considered unconstitutional. In Ontario, section 51 of the Education Act allows a student to receive whatever religious instruction the student's parent wishes (or that the student wishes, if the student is an adult). Furthermore, clause (c) of section 264(1) still requires teachers to nurture in students, among other things, "respect for religion and the principles of Judaeo-Christian morality." This clause is, however, unlikely to be enforced today.

In fact, in Ontario, the mandatory recitation of the Lord's Prayer in public schools ceased after the Ontario Court of Appeal ruled in the 1988 case *Zylberberg v. Sudbury Board of Education (Director)* (1988 CanLII 189 [ONCA]) that making students recite the prayer violated the Charter of Rights and Freedoms.[6] The following year, a similar case in British Columbia led that province's Supreme Court to decide the same way as the Ontario court. As a result, the British Columbia School Act was changed to eliminate

---

6 The four judges who wrote the majority opinion didn't explicitly rule out the system adopted by the Toronto Board of Education, which, in place of the Lord's Prayer, drew on a book of readings from a wide variety of religious traditions. But they expressed no opinion, one way or another, on the constitutionality of this system.

the required recitation of the Lord's Prayer, which was replaced with a rule that all public schools must be run on "strictly secular and non-sectarian" (that is, non-religious) principles and that "the highest morality must be inculcated, but no religious dogma or creed is to be taught" (ss. 76[1] and 76[2]). In general, since public schools are run by the government, and the government must respect the Charter of Rights and Freedoms, all the remaining laws that allow religious exercises (except in separate schools) could one day be found unconstitutional.

In separate schools, students have traditionally received instruction in the faith of the religious group that supports the school. Depending on the province, the school may be able to require that students take part in prayers and religious services. In 2014, however, the Ontario Superior Court decided in *Erazo v. Dufferin-Peel Catholic District School Board* (2014 ONSC 2072 [CanLII]) that a boy who went to a Catholic school but was not Catholic himself didn't have to participate in any of the school's religious activities. So this requirement may also be on its way out.

Of course, if you *want* to pray at school, you always have the right to do so, provided you don't do so in a way that disturbs the lesson or other students and teachers.

In short, the school system in Canada tries to keep you safe, to teach you to respect other people's rights (and other people to respect yours), and to give you a reasonable number of choices. We think it's ironic, though, that a system that is supposed to be teaching you skills you will need as an adult still tends to make it difficult for you to make these choices yourself, independently of your parents, even once you reach high school. We also find it strange that a multicultural country such as Canada, where people of any and all religions, including those who have no religion, are supposed to be equal, still has religious schools—but only Christian ones—that are paid for by public money. What sort of message does this deliver to students (and to adults)?

GOING TO WORK

Getting your first job is a big milestone in your life. Not only does it provide you with steady money, but it also gives you a chance to gain valuable experience and become more independent.

But your relationship with the person or company you work for is not a private one. There's a whole branch of the law that deals with the rights and duties of employers and employees. It's called *labour law,* and it covers matters such as:

- the minimum amount that workers must be paid

- the way in which employees are paid

- how much time workers are allowed for eating meals, taking breaks, and having a vacation

- the health and safety of workers on the job

- protection from discrimination because of gender, age, race, or any other reason (this includes the principle of equal pay for equal work)

- trade unions—associations that enable workers to negotiate wages and working conditions with their employer

All provinces and territories have labour laws, and these laws can differ quite a bit from one place to another. But they also have certain things in common.

Everyone Has Rights at Work

Before we talk about young people's rights under labour law, let's make it clear that *all* people, regardless of age, have rights at work. Although there are special rules about what jobs a young person can do, and at what age, once you do get a job, you generally have the same rights and responsibilities as an adult when it comes to things like work safety, entitlement to pay, vacation and sick leave, your performance at work, and other issues connected with your relationship with the employer.

Once you start working—or even before you get a job—it's a good idea to become familiar with the rights and responsibilities that employees have in the province or territory where you live. General labour law and workers' rights are beyond the scope of this book, but you can find information about your rights as an employee on the website of your province's Ministry of Labour or a similar government agency. Also, if you work in a unionized job, you can participate in the activities of the union and get to know the terms and conditions that it has agreed on with your employer, which are laid out in a document called a collective agreement.

If an employer violates one of your rights (for example, if you are not paid, if you are fired for no apparent reason, or if your boss sexually harasses you), there are government offices that you can complain to, such as Employment Standards in Alberta or the *Commission des normes, de l'équité, de la santé et de la sécurité du travail* in Québec. You should report a complaint as soon as possible after the incident, as there will be rules about how much time you have to do so—and, the longer you wait, the harder it will be to prove that the incident happened. If you belong to a union, you can consult with it about filing a *grievance* (that is, a formal complaint), and the union will help you do this. Otherwise, before you report a complaint, you should try to find out what the law says about the rule you think your employer has broken. But you may need to get help from a lawyer.[1]

---

1 For information on workers' rights by province and territory and links to relevant government legislation and web pages, see "Employment and Labour Standards," on the *Workershelp.ca* website: http://www.workershelp.ca/employmentstandards.asp. As the page points out, "Determining your rights under employment standards legislation can be a difficult task. It requires careful reading of the appropriate section(s) of legislation and corresponding regulations. In addition there are numerous exceptions and exemptions that may need to be considered." This is why you may need to get some legal help.

Child Labour Laws

On top of the laws that apply to all workers and employers, there are child labour laws that lay down rules for hiring youth. One purpose of these laws is to protect you from doing work considered too dangerous, too physically demanding, or otherwise inappropriate for a child or teenager, as well as to prevent exploitation of children by adults. Another is to make sure work doesn't interfere with your education.

FACT FILE Child Labour

It's a long time ago, but before the first child labour laws were passed, many children worked from an early age, often under appalling conditions. If you were born into a poor, working-class family in the nineteenth or early twentieth century, you could expect to start work when you were as young as 7 years old to help support yourself and your family. You might easily end up in a mine or in a factory doing dirty, repetitive, and possibly dangerous work for very little pay. For a long time, not many adults seemed to care that young people were being treated this way: it just seemed normal. After all, working-class adults had to work in much the same conditions. Eventually, though, people began to ask whether it was right to exploit children in this way and to deny them a chance to get a basic education. The first Canadian laws against child labour, such as Nova Scotia's 1873 limits on children working in mines, focused mainly on keeping young people out of dangerous industrial jobs at an overly young age. As provinces passed compulsory school attendance laws and people started caring more about children's well-being, child labour laws became stricter.

The conditions that existed back at the start of the twentieth century would be impossible in Canada today. Yet, even in this well-off country, a great many children live in poverty. And in many poorer countries, children still labour, sometimes in harsh conditions, just to help put food on the table.

 From what age may I work?

One of the main ways in which the law attempts to protect you is by simply laying down a minimum age for starting to work. In the vast majority of provinces and territories, the hiring of youth is forbidden or restricted until the child reaches a certain age (see table 3). Working ages are not always absolute: most provinces allow those under the minimum age to get at least some kinds of jobs with permission from a parent and/or a provincial government official. In this matter, Canadian law is relatively tolerant. In some countries, young people are prohibited from working until they are somewhere in their teens, and it is all but impossible to hire a young person who is below the minimum age.

Table 3 Minimum age for employment

Employment age	Relevant legal provision(s)
Alberta. Under 15 generally requires written parental permission and approval of the Director of Employment Standards; in some jobs, possible from 12 with only written parental permission	Employment Standards Code, s. 65(2); Alberta Regulation 14/97: Employment Standards Regulation, ss. 51(a) and 52(1)
British Columbia. Under 15 requires written parental permission; under 12 also requires permission of the Director of Employment Standards	Employment Standards Act, ss. 9(1) and 9(2)
Manitoba. Under 16 requires a permit issued by the Director of Employment Standards on receipt of an application signed by the employer and a parent; permit for under 12 given only in special circumstances	Employment Standards Code, s. 83
New Brunswick. Under 14 restricted from many kinds of work unless a parent consents and the Director of Employment Standards issues a permit	Employment Standards Act, ss. 40 and 41(1)

Employment age	Relevant legal provision(s)
Newfoundland and Labrador. Under 16 requires written permission of a parent; under 14 restricted from certain kinds of work	Labour Standards Act, ss. 45, 46(c), and 48(1)
Northwest Territories. Under 16, some kinds of work require approval of Employment Standards Officer	Employment Standards Act, ss. 1, 44, and 45
Nova Scotia. Under 16 restricted from many kinds of work; some exceptions if employed by a family member; further restrictions for under 14	Labour Standards Code, s. 68
Nunavut. Under 17, construction work requires written approval of Labour Standards Officer	Employment of Young Persons Regulations, ss. 1 and 2
Ontario. 14 for most jobs; 15, 16, or 18 for certain occupations	Occupational Health and Safety Act—different regulations on industrial establishments (such as construction projects), mines, and window cleaning
Prince Edward Island. Under 16 may not be employed in construction	Youth Employment Act, ss. 1(e) and 5

Employment age	Relevant legal provision(s)
Québec. Under 14 requires written parental permission	Act Respecting Labour Standards, s. 84.3, para. 1
Saskatchewan. 16; from 14 if the youth completes a Young Worker Readiness Certificate Course and has written permission of parent; the Director of Employment Standards permitted to excuse a young person from work restrictions but may also set conditions	Conditions of Employment Regulations, ss. 9.1(1) and 9.1(2), 9.3(1), 9.4, and 9.5
Yukon. Under 17 can be restricted from some kinds of work by the regulations; Employment Standards Board may set further conditions	Employment Standards Act 18(2)(f) and 18(6)

To be employed by the federal government, you must be at least 17, except in an occupation allowed by regulations, subject to any conditions governing employment in that occupation (Canada Labour Code, s. 179).

Besides minimum age, there are many other rules that limit when, where, and under what conditions you can work. For example, jobs in construction or heavy industry (such as welding), as well as jobs that require you to lift heavy loads, will often be off limits until you're 16 to 18. These restrictions, which differ from one province or territory to another, can range from bans on working during school hours to rules that set specific minimum ages for specific professions to restrictions that say you can do only relatively light work. In Prince Edward Island, for instance, the Youth Employment Act says that, until you are 16:

- You can't be employed in a job that is or is likely to be harmful to your health or safety or harmful to your moral or physical development, nor can you be employed in any construction-related jobs (ss. 4 and 5).

- You can't work between 11:00 p.m. and 7:00 a.m. or during normal school hours (except in a vocational training or apprenticeship program) or for more than three hours on any school day, eight hours on any day other than a school day, or forty hours in the whole week (s. 6[1]). Exceptions can be made by the provincial inspector of labour standards if your parents consent and the inspector thinks that the work won't interfere with your education and school attendance (ss. 6[2] and 6[3]).

Note that the Youth Employment Act doesn't apply to work that is part of your study program at a trade school, nor does it apply if you work in a family business that employs only family members (s. 2).

There are also a few practical obstacles to consider. The fact is that, even if it's legal to work below the standard working age with your parents' and/or the government's permission, the paperwork involved means that relatively few people may consider hiring you. In addition, compulsory school attendance means that you can't usually get a full-time job until you graduate from high school. And, of course, you won't be a candidate for some jobs simply because you don't yet have the level of education or training that the job requires.

 What about working in family businesses?

One limitation of child labour laws is that they generally cover only *paid employment,* carried out under formal hire, as opposed to helping someone for free. So a young person working in a parent's business may have no legal protection. In Alberta, for instance, employment standards legislation specifically exempts a business owner's family members from its rules. Unpaid labour performed by children is especially common on family farms, and yet laws covering the safety of agricultural workers typically don't cover children who provide free work to their family. It is also legal in some places for children to drive tractors before they can legally drive a car, as long as, for example, they don't drive along a public road.

Moreover, even when laws about workplace safety apply to farms, officials may be reluctant to enforce these laws when it comes to family members. In 2014, following a complaint about underage labour, an inspection of a Saskatchewan farm confirmed that the owners' two daughters, aged 8 and 10, were working in the chicken processing plant, as were several local teenagers under the age of 16—in violation of the provincial Occupational Health and Safety Act. The parents duly received an order forbidding them to allow anyone under 16 to work in the

plant. After the parents protested, however, the Saskatchewan Labour minister decided that the children (but not
the other youth) could continue to work in the plant, as it
was considered part of the family farm.

The law assumes that parents will not force their children to do unpaid work that could put them in danger or
be so heavy or demanding as to amount to exploitation. The
question then arises about where to draw the line between
reasonable duties and exploitation, or what the law calls
"unjust enrichment"—a situation in which a person profits
at someone else's expense. For example, in *Antrobus v. Antrobus* (2009 BCSC 1341 [CanLII]), the BC Supreme Court ruled
in favour of a daughter who had spent her teen years and
much of her adulthood cooking meals, doing heavy house-
work, and helping out in shops and later on farms that her
parents owned, all for nothing in return. In other words, the
daughter was doing the sort of work that would normally
be done by hired help. In the court's judgment, this was a
case of exploitation, and the parents were ordered to pay
their daughter damages of $190,000 (on appeal, this was
reduced to $100,000).

Not all hard work qualifies as exploitation, however. In
a more recent case, *McDonald v. McDonald* (2017 BCCA 255
[CanLII]), three adult siblings were angry when, several
years after their father died, they learned that their parents, who owned a sizable dairy farm, had transferred most
of the shares in the farm to their brother. They took the
case to court, arguing that their relatively meagre inheritance would not adequately compensate for the hard work

they had done on the farm when growing up. In making this claim, they relied partly on the *Antrobus* decision. Initially, the trial judge agreed and awarded each of them $350,000 from the estate minus the value of their existing inheritance. The BC Court of Appeal overturned the earlier decision, however, ruling that the unpaid work they had done on the farm as teenagers, even if hard and unpaid, was not sufficiently unusual or demanding to be considered exploitation.

 What about babysitting or other self-employment?

Laws regulating child labour typically don't apply to occasional work, such as babysitting or mowing a neighbour's lawn, that a young person might do to earn some money. Subject to certain conditions, young people are also generally allowed to earn money by performing, whether as singers, musicians, or actors. In particular, if you want to have a performance career, your parents and employers must make sure that you still receive an education. You can also start your own business at any age, provided it doesn't interfere with your education and as long as operating the business doesn't involve actions (such as signing contracts) that are beyond your legal capacity as a minor. To incorporate a business company, however, or to sit on the board of directors of an incorporated company, you must be at least 18 (Canada Business Corporations Act, ss. 5[2][a] and 105[1][a]).

Minimum Wage

Minimum wage is the least amount of money that an employer is allowed to pay an employee. As we write, it ranges from $11.06 an hour in Saskatchewan to $15.00 an hour in Alberta. Although, as a general rule, everyone who is hired for regular work must be paid at least this wage, in Ontario there is an odd exception that affects young workers' pay. The general minimum wage in Ontario is currently $14.00 an hour—but a different minimum wage applies to several groups, including students under the age of 18 who work no more than 28 hours a week when school is in session or during a school break or summer holidays. Their minimum wage is $13.15 an hour. It's not that big a difference, but students over 18 working under the exact same conditions must get full minimum wage. Doesn't this seem like discrimination?

It seems that lawmakers presume that, because young people under 18 must have less need for money because they're supposedly being supported by their parents. However, some young people already support themselves or help to support their family. Also, this idea goes against the principle that you don't pay people on the basis of how much money you think they need; rather, you pay them on the basis of the work they do. The same kind of reasoning was once used to justify paying women less than men. Until equal pay for equal work laws were passed, many employers conveniently assumed that, while a man needed money to support a family, a woman could be supported by a man and therefore didn't need to be paid as much. Today, we know that this is wrong. Men and women should be paid the same, and so should youth and adults.

 Can I keep the money I earn?

It used to be common for parents to hire their children out and then use their earnings to help support the family. The idea that parents are entitled to the earnings of a child who has not yet come of age took hold in the United States, where, in most states, a minor's earnings generally belong to his or her parents. However, we have found no Canadian law that explicitly upholds such a principle. In fact, in 1923, in *Haas v. Nyholm* (1923 CanLII 300 [SKQB])—a case involving a father who was trying to lay claim to income earned by his underage son—a Saskatchewan superior court ruled: "A parent cannot, in that capacity, nor in His own right, recover the wages earned by a minor child." As the judge further stated: "There would appear to be no authority for the proposition that a parent has the right to hire out his children who are under age living with and supported by the parent." Presumably, then, in Canada, money you earn is legally your own property, not that of your parents.

As we saw in chapter 1, in Québec, article 220 of the Civil Code specifically entitles you to manage the money you have earned through your work, as well as allowances given to you for meeting your usual needs. However, the article also says that if your revenues are "considerable," or "where justified by the circumstances" (for example, if your parents feel that you're wasting your money), a court may decide how much of your money you will be allowed to manage yourself.

So much for the letter of the law. In practice, because parents are sometimes called upon to *manage* a minor child's property (including financial assets), they may simply assume that they have a right to decide what is done with it—that they somehow "own" the property. This is especially tempting when children earn substantial sums of money. In British Columbia, the law gives some income protection to children who work in the entertainment industry by requiring the government to hold part of their earnings for them until they reach the age of majority (19, in BC). According to BC Regulation 396/95, which pertains to the Employment Standards Act, if a child under 15 who works in the film, radio, video, or television industry earns more than $2,000 on a production, the employer must give 25 percent of his or her earnings over $2,000 to the Public Guardian and Trustee to hold in trust for the child (s. 45.14). The same goes for a child who works in the live entertainment industry and earns more than $1,000 in a single week (s. 45.20).

FACT FILE   Coogan Laws

The BC law that requires the government to hold some of the earnings of a child performer in trust for the child until he or she turns 19 is a Canadian example of what is known in the United States as a "Coogan law." In most American states, parents are entitled to a child's earnings, as long as the child is still a minor. Several states (currently California, Louisiana, New Mexico, and New York), however, require that some or all of the money earned by child actors or performers be set aside for the child. These are called "Coogan" laws, named after Jackie Coogan, a child star of the silent film era. By the time he turned 21, Coogan had earned an estimated $3 to $4 million—but his mother and stepfather had spent almost all of his money. Jackie sued for the remaining $250,000, but, after court costs, he ended up with only $126,000. This prompted the state of California to pass the Child Actor's Bill, which came to be known as the "Coogan Act" or the "Coogan Law." In 1939, when the law was enacted, it required only that 15 percent of a child actor's earnings be protected in a trust. In 2000, a change to the law came into force, giving more protection to such earnings. While section 7500 of the California Family Code still says that parents are entitled to "the services and earnings" of an unemancipated minor child, it makes an exception for income from occupations mentioned in section 6750—"artistic and creative services," as well as sports. This money belongs to the child, not to his or her parents—and, as an added safeguard, sections 6752 and 6753 require the employer to deposit 15 percent of the earnings into a "Coogan Trust Account."

It seems a shame that, while California has taken the trouble to give children ownership of the money they earn through acting or other talent-related work, parents are still entitled to the money earned by young people through other kinds of work. The reasoning is that, because parents are obligated to support their children, any money the children earn should be given to the parents by way of compensation—but, because child stars often earn a great deal more money than their parents could possibly spend on their support, entitling parents to all of this income would be unfair. Yet parents have a *duty* to support their children, and we wonder why parents should have a right to be paid for doing their duty. Ultimately, a duty is a *moral* obligation (though it may also be a legal one), and people don't usually expect to be reimbursed for making good on their moral responsibilities. The argument that parents are entitled to the fruits of their children's labour finally seems to rest on the antiquated view that parents "own" their children—so whatever the child possesses is actually the parents' property. In other words, it denies that children are independent individuals who, like adults, have a right to keep what they earn.

Elsewhere in Canada, ACTRA, the union to which Canadian film, television, and radio artists belong, administers a Minors' Trust through its Performers' Rights Society. Once a minor's earnings reach $5,000 (and beyond), 25 percent of the earnings are deposited in the trust, much as in BC, and held in safekeeping until the child comes of age. This isn't a "law," in the sense of a statute. It's a contractual provision that the union negotiated—perhaps because the law wasn't doing enough to protect children's earnings.

So what are we to make of Canada's child labour laws? Like labour laws in general, they place a lot of emphasis on protecting people from exploitation. This is because employers are the ones with the power. Much like parents, they expect their employees not only to do the work they've been hired (that is, told) to do but also to behave in certain ways. So labour laws exist to make sure that employees are treated fairly. As we've pointed out, though, these laws apply almost entirely to "regular" employment, when one person is formally hired by another. When it comes to family labour, the law usually intervenes only when a complaint is made or a case is brought to court.

What do you think? Should the law do more to regulate how much work children can be obliged to do for their parents, and of what sort and at what age? Or, to put it another way, should labour law do more to recognize that "work" doesn't always involve paid employment? As it is, the law seems to assume that, as long as children are minors, parents have a right to act as their employers—but it doesn't offer children much protection from these employers, unless they do something pretty extreme. And there's no such thing as a children's union, at least not in the sense of an organization that would work to protect young people's rights as family workers. We also wonder whether the law is too swift to assume that, because parents are expected to "protect" their children, they will automatically give them the sort of protection that the law gives to paid workers. But maybe these are two different kinds of protection.

LOVE, SEX, AND MARRIAGE

As we have seen, except when a fairly serious problem arises, the law is generally reluctant to interfere in personal relationships. So you might think that it would steer clear of sex—which is, after all, the most intimate of personal relationships. Yet sex is a subject about which most societies have seen fit to make rules. In Canada, most of these rules are found in the Criminal Code, and there are strict penalties for breaking them. In criminalizing certain activities that relate to sex, the law aims to protect people from being forced into intimate behaviour they do not want, from acts they may not be physically and/or emotionally ready for, and from other actions that could harm them in some way or that involve exploitation. The law also lays down rules about the circumstances under which two people can marry, as well as about the rights and responsibilities that marriage brings with it.

Although the law is not supposed to pass judgment on private morality, it does seek to protect what the Criminal

Code calls "public morals." In other words, it tries to outlaw activities that, in the opinion of lawmakers, could tend to corrupt moral standards, including those that relate to sexual behaviour. But this is an area in which the rules can get controversial. Quite apart from the fact that social attitudes toward sex shift over time, private morality differs a lot from one person to another. So how do we decide what moral standards the "public" (that is, everyone who lives in a country) should have? This is a very difficult question, and the best we can do here is tell you what the law regards as unacceptable.

No Means No: The Need for Consent

Do you have a right to have sex? Only under some conditions. In order for sexual contact to be legal, both people involved must consent to it. This means that your partner must make it clear that he or she wants to engage in sexual activity with you; otherwise, you have no right to continue. It also means that you must always respect your partner's wishes and never, under any circumstances, force anything on your partner that he or she does not want. Forcing anyone of any age to engage in sexual activity against their will is a crime, called sexual assault. Under section 271 of the Criminal Code, the penalty for sexual assault can be as high as ten years in prison—up to fourteen years if the victim is under 16.

Sexual assault includes not only rape and other forced intercourse but also unwanted kissing, petting, or any touching that could be seen as sexual. It doesn't matter if the person you are with began getting intimate with you willingly. If he or she says to stop at any point, you must do so. Furthermore, according to section 153.1(3) of the Criminal Code, in order to be able to give legal consent (and to continue to do so), your partner must be mentally competent—that is, he or she must be able to make decisions. Someone who is drugged or extremely drunk is in no position to say yes or no. It is an especially serious offence to deliberately drug someone or otherwise render someone unconscious or incapable of resistance in order to have sex with the person. Under section 246 of the Criminal Code, committing such an offence could result in life imprisonment.

It also doesn't matter whether you already know someone and the two of you perhaps share a mutual attraction. If you force this person to have sex with you, this is rape. More specifically, it's what is often called "date rape" (or sometimes "acquaintance rape"). Date rape may involve giving a drug to the victim or getting the person very drunk and then having sex with him or her—which, as we just mentioned, is a very serious crime. At the same time, as section 33.1 of the Criminal Code makes clear, being intoxicated yourself is *not* a defence against criminal charges. This is underscored in section 153.1(5), according to which you can't argue that you were drunk or high, and so you *thought* your partner had consented. As the law sees it, if someone chose to become intoxicated, that person is still held responsible for their actions.

The Age of Consent

The law puts strict limits on the age you must be before someone may engage in any form of sexual activity with you—not merely sexual intercourse but also any other behaviour of a sexual nature (including hugging or kissing that is clearly more than just a friendly show of affection). Before you reach the age of 12, the law considers that you are neither physically nor emotionally mature enough for sexual activity. Until that age, you cannot consent to sexual contact of any sort, and someone who forces it on you is guilty of child abuse.[1] Otherwise, in Canada, the "age of consent" for sexual activity is set at 16. This means that, until you reach the age of 16, you are not legally able to consent to sexual activity, and a person who initiates or attempts to initiate sexual activity with you is guilty of a crime, according to section 151 of the Criminal Code. (These rules do not apply if the two people are married— although, as we will see below, you cannot marry until you are at least 16.)

The law recognizes, however, that young people some-times have sexual relationships with each other, and so it makes some exceptions when young partners are close in age. Thus, according to sections 150.1(2) and (2.1), a person who is 12 or 13 may consent to sexual activity with someone

---

1 This does not apply, however, if both participants are under the age of 12. Young children sometimes "mess around" with each other, partly out of curiosity, but until a child turns 12, he or she cannot be held criminally responsible for anything.

who is less than two years older, and a person who is 14 or 15 may consent when the other person is less than five years older—provided, in both cases, that the older person is not attempting to exploit the younger one or take advantage of a relationship of authority or dependence.

Although the age of sexual consent is normally 16, in some situations, which the Criminal Code considers to be "sexual exploitation," the age is 18. Until you reach the age of 18, you can't legally consent to sexual activity with someone on whom you are dependent or who stands in a position of authority or trust toward you. This can mean a teacher, coach, camp counsellor, employer, family member, foster parent, doctor, or similar person. You must also be 18 to consent if the sexual act is for the purpose of prostitution or pornography, if you are paid to engage in it, or if it involves some other kind of exploitative relationship. In addition, it is illegal to use the Internet to communicate with a young person in order to commit a sexual offence against him or her.

These rules are meant for the protection of young people. But there is one strange exception to the standard age of consent. In the case of *anal* sex, the age of consent is set at 18. It is actually a *crime* to have anal sex unless both participants are 18 or older (or are husband and wife) and do so in private (Criminal Code, s. 159). This discriminatory rule has no protective value for youth and is apparently an out-dated morality law, one that has been found unconstitutional by the highest courts in Ontario (1995), Québec (1998), British

Columbia (2003), and Nova Scotia (2006).[2] Two bills are currently before the House of Commons (C-32 and C-39) that would repeal section 159.

"Sexting" and Online Harassment

Sexting, or using the Internet to share images of a person that are meant to cause sexual arousal or excitement, has become a popular activity in recent years. Sharing a picture of someone who is naked or semi-naked and/or is engaged in a sexual action is legal as long as both the person in the picture and whoever is taking or sharing the picture are 18 or older and as long as everyone involved in creating and sharing the picture consents. If the person in the picture is *under* 18, however, sexting is legally considered child pornography, and taking and distributing the picture is a criminal offence.

With respect to the creation and distribution of child pornography, however, the Supreme Court has recognized an exception if two young people take pictures of themselves in an explicit sexual act together. For this to be legal, however, they must both consent to creating the picture, and they must *both* be in the picture and create it together. In addition, the picture must not show any illegal sexual

2 *R. v. Blake* (2003 BCCA 525 [CanLII]); *R. v. T.C.F.* (2006 NSCA 42 [CanLII]); *R. v. C.M.* (1995 CanLII 8924 [OCCA]); and *R. c. Roy* (1998 CanLII 12775 [QCCA]). In a 2002 Alberta court case, a lower court also ruled that section 159 was unconstitutional (*R. v. Roth,* 2002 ABQB 145 [CanLII]).

activity, and they *must keep it to themselves*.[3] If they send the image along to anyone else, or if the image shows only *one* of them, then the sexting is considered child pornography, which is a serious crime. Even if you are under 18, it is not illegal to create a provocative image of yourself alone (a selfie), but, again, you must keep it to yourself—that is, share it with no one, not even your partner.

As numerous young people have discovered, one problem with sexting is that, while you may think that someone with whom you've shared a sexually provocative picture will keep it private, that person may still choose to share it with others. If, without your knowledge or permission, someone shares private pictures that he or she took of you, this is considered a form of online harassment (or cyberbullying), and the same is true if someone spreads information about your sexual behaviour online. Although the person who shares the picture or the information may not realize it, he or she may be committing a crime—for example, under section 162 of the Criminal Code (which deals with voyeurism), or section 163.1 (which concerns child pornography), or section 264 (which defines criminal harassment). So, quite apart from the situation you're in, the other person could be in serious trouble.

If a picture of you ends up on the Internet or otherwise shared, or if someone writes lewd things about you

---

3 This is often called the "private use exception." The Supreme Court first defined this exception in 2001, in *R. v. Sharpe* (2001 SCC 2 [CanLII]). Certain refinements were made to the definition in 2015, in *R. v. Barabash* (2015 SCC 29 [CanLII]).

or attacks you online, you can ask the website to take down the picture or remove the post. If the picture or post is especially offensive, it might be best to have a lawyer threaten the poster or the website with a court order or even to press criminal charges, if there are grounds for doing so. In particular, if someone ever threatens to harm you in some way if you don't allow that person to have sex with you or share sexually provocative images of you, you should get help. As we mentioned in chapter 4, threats—of whatever sort—that reasonably cause someone to fear for his or her safety (or the safety of someone he or she knows) are a crime under section 264 of the Criminal Code.

Getting Married

According to Canada's 1867 Constitution Act, laws governing marriage are a federal responsibility, but provinces and territories can pass laws regarding the "solemnization" of marriage, including the age at which someone can get a marriage licence. In 2001, when the Parliament amended the Civil Marriage Act—which legalized same-sex marriage throughout the country—it set the minimum age for marriage at 16 (s. 2.2). So, no matter where you live, it's impossible to get married before you turn 16.[4] In practical

---

4 Even though the minimum age was set at 16 quite some time ago, provinces and territories haven't necessarily amended their legislation accordingly. For example, section 29(2) of the British Columbia Marriage Act still states: "If, on application to the Supreme Court, a marriage is shown to be expedient and in the interests of the parties,

terms, however, until you are a legal adult (18 or 19 years of age, depending on the province), you generally cannot get a marriage licence without the written permission of your parents or guardians.

For example, according to section 5 of Ontario's Marriage Act, if you are under the age of 18 (that is, if you are 16 or 17), you will need the written consent of both your parents in order to marry, unless you have already been married and were widowed or divorced. If your parents are living apart or if one (or both) of them is dead or is otherwise incapable of granting legal consent, permission may be given by the parent who has custody or by a lawful guardian, as the case may be. If the person who has the power to give consent is unavailable or arbitrarily refuses to give consent, then, under section 6(1), you can apply to a judge to dispense with consent. If all else fails, section 10 allows you to ask the government minister responsible for the administration of the Marriage Act to issue a marriage licence.

In Québec, the law is a little different. There, if you wish to get married before you turn 18, you will need the consent of a court, according to article 373 of the Civil Code. In this case, you can apply to the court yourself for this authorization, and the judge will then summon your parents or guardians to give their opinion—but their consent as such is not necessary.

---

the court may, in its discretion, make an order authorizing the solemnization of and the issuing of a licence for the marriage of any person under 16 years of age." This is by no means the only example—but all such provisions are now invalid.

If you applied to a court to dispense with parental consent (or if, in Québec, a judge were to override your parents' objections), you could be pretty sure that the judge would not do so lightly. He or she would want to be convinced that you are mature enough to be ready for marriage, that you understand the responsibilities that marriage entails, and that you are not making a hasty or frivolous decision but have thought through all the consequences. When two young people want to get married because the girl is pregnant, the fact of a pregnancy alone will probably not persuade a judge to give consent, if he or she feels that one or both of them is not yet mature enough to take this step.

If you do end up marrying under the age of majority, you gain all the rights and responsibilities of any other married person. Today, husbands and wives are equal in the eyes of the law: they owe each other mutual respect, the willingness to engage in a sexual relationship, and faithfulness. (These duties cannot be enforced, but not fulfilling them can be cause for divorce.) They must respect each other's legal rights and are generally expected to support each other in times of need and allow each other to live in the family home, even if only one of them owns it. If you marry while you are still a minor, you also acquire many of the rights of a legal adult. Your parents no longer have authority over you (but, depending on the province, you may also lose the right to their support), and you may now perform many legal actions that a minor normally cannot. This change in status is permanent: it persists even if you divorce or are widowed before you reach the age of majority.

Forced Marriage

In Canada today, it's up to each person to decide when to get married and to whom. In other words, marriage is a matter of individual choice. This seems natural to most of us because we think of getting married as something people do when they've fallen in love, and only we can decide whether we love someone. In many cultures, though, parents are the ones who choose their children's marriage partner, sometimes with the help of other adult family members. This is called arranged marriage, and it reflects a different way of thinking about marriage, one that has less to do with notions of love and individual freedom and more to do with familial duty. In fact, for a long time, this system was quite common among the aristocracy in Europe and Britain—and traces of parental permission survive in our old custom that a man must ask a woman's father for her hand in marriage.

In Canada, it isn't illegal for parents to arrange a marriage, as long as the two people getting married are happy with the arrangement and freely agree to it. What is illegal, however, is *forced* marriage, in which one or both young persons are pressured into marrying or even compelled by threats to do so. In Canada, forcing someone to get married is a federal crime. According to section 293.1 of the Criminal Code, "Everyone who celebrates, aids or participates in a marriage rite or ceremony knowing that one of the persons being married is marrying against their will is guilty of an indictable offence and liable to imprisonment for a term not exceeding five years." In this context, people who "aid" a marriage include parents or other family members who attempt to force a marriage. In addition, some of the methods that could be used in such an attempt—such as beating the person, unlawfully confining the person, or threatening him or her with injury or death—are illegal in themselves.

Of course, many parents hint around or even openly suggest that it's time for one of their children to get married. For example, some parents feel that living together without getting married is morally wrong, and so they may try to convince the couple to get married. Although, for the most part, this sort of thing doesn't happen before a young person is already a legal adult, sometimes—especially if the girl is pregnant—parents may put serious pressure on young people to get married, even if one or both of them is still a minor. Any young person who feels that he or she is being coerced or compelled to marry should regard this as a high-risk situation and seek help. Because the law considers it essential that both partners freely agree to a marriage, if someone is forced into marrying, the person can later ask a court to annul the marriage (that is, to declare it invalid). Assuming that the person asking for an annulment can provide convincing evidence that he or she got married as the result of threats or undue pressure, the annulment should be granted. If for some reason it isn't, the person can ask the court for a divorce.

There can, at times, be a delicate line between an arranged marriage and a forced marriage. If your parents immigrated to Canada from a country in which arranged marriages are the custom, they may wish to choose a marriage partner for you from their home country and may even want to send you abroad for the purpose of getting married. Provided that you are a legal adult and are perfectly content with the plan, there is nothing wrong with consenting to this arrangement. If you are underage, however, the situation is a little different.

According to section 273.3 of the Criminal Code, if you are under 18 and are "ordinarily resident in Canada" (that is, if this is where you normally live), it is a crime for anyone to take you out of the country with the intention of committing certain crimes, many of which relate to sexual activity. So, for instance, you cannot be taken to another country and forced into prostitution. Under this same section—specifically, paragraph (1)(d)—it is also illegal for your parents to send you abroad for a forced marriage (which, as we mentioned above, is prohibited under s. 293.1) or for marriage at all, if you are under 16 (prohibited under s. 293.2). If you are still a minor and you suspect that your family may be planning to take you to another country in order to force you to get married, you should get in touch with the police or your local Children's Aid Society or other child protection agency. If need be, they could take you into protective custody (something we'll talk about in the next chapter). In an emergency situation, you could take the radical step of destroying your passport, which would at least delay an attempt to take you out of Canada.

In some such cases, the plan might be to have you return to Canada at some point after you're married, so that your spouse can later move here as well. But it might also be that your parents intend to have you live in the other country (although, if you're already a Canadian citizen, they cannot legally force you to leave the country permanently).[5] If, in the end, you do end up in another country and are a Canadian citizen or permanent resident, you should contact the Canadian embassy or consulate there and explain your situation. Give them your full name, along with information about your citizenship and where you have lived in Canada, and show them any Canadian identification you may have with you (SIN card, health card, passport, citizenship card, driver's licence). They may be able to help you.

Birth Control and Abortion

Bringing a child into the world is a huge responsibility. So it is only sensible that, when having sex, a person of any age who is not fully prepared to raise a child should take steps to avoid an unwanted pregnancy. A young person's legal right to have access to birth control depends on what kind of contraceptives he or she wants to use:

---

5 Under section 6 of the Charter of Rights and Freedoms, all Canadian citizens have a right to reside in Canada, as well as leave and return to the country. But if you're still a minor and have only permanent resident status, your parents could actually apply on your behalf to have you relinquish that status. (They cannot apply to have your citizenship revoked, however: only a citizen himself or herself can renounce citizenship, and you must be 18 to do so.) If you think your parents may be planning to have your permanent residency revoked, you should definitely consult a lawyer.

- Condoms can be bought at any age, and some sexual health clinics or HIV centres distribute them for free. Many high schools also sell them from dispensers in the washrooms, though in this case there's no guarantee that the condom will be fresh enough for reliable use.

- The birth control pill must be prescribed to a woman by a doctor. Usually, there should be no problem once you're 16; under that age, the doctor may still prescribe the pill if he or she thinks you're mature enough. (The fact that you're trying to prevent an unwanted pregnancy will, we would hope, show that you are indeed mature enough.) Before going to any doctor or clinic to get a prescription for the pill, make sure they are willing to keep it secret from your parents if you don't want them to know about it.

- Emergency contraception (the "morning-after pill") works by preventing an egg from being fertilized by a sperm very shortly after sex. Because it's not as effective as normal birth control pills, it shouldn't be used as regular contraception but only in the case that you have just failed to use adequate protection and think you might get pregnant. There's no age restriction for buying the morning-after pill; it is readily available over the counter in drugstores in most provinces.

Whereas birth control is the *prevention* of pregnancy, abortion is the termination of a pregnancy that has already begun. Abortion is a controversial issue. While a majority of Canadians now see it as a woman's right to decide whether to have an abortion, this was not always the case, and there are still those who think ending a pregnancy is immoral. The decision to have an abortion or to refuse to do so is up to the woman: the child's father can neither forbid her to have one nor compel her to. If you do get pregnant, you should get information from a reliable and neutral expert about what abortion involves before making a decision.

Abortion used to be a crime except when it was performed for certain health reasons, and the ban on abortions—section 287 of the Criminal Code—has never been formally repealed. However, it is no longer valid, thanks to the Supreme Court's decision in *R. v. Morgentaler* (1988 CanLII 90 [SCC]), in which the Court ruled that this law violated a woman's right to liberty, as guaranteed by section 7 of the Charter of Rights and Freedoms. As a result, abortion is legal across the country and may be performed at any time during the pregnancy without criminal charges, although the vast majority of abortions occur when the fetus is no more than 12 weeks old.

Q Where can I get an abortion?

Although abortion is legal everywhere in Canada, access to it varies. Some provinces have more locations that provide abortions than others, and rules that specify the conditions under which doctors may provide an abortion differ from one province to another as well. Generally, there are far more abortion providers in big cities than in rural areas. Abortions are performed in some public hospitals; there, you can obtain them for free, at least if you're a resident of the province and have a provincial health card. However, in places where the local culture tends to be conservative, hospital staff may be reluctant to perform abortions and might encourage you to talk to someone, who would then try to convince you not to have it done. There are also "abortion counselling" services that try to appear neutral but that actually exist to persuade women not to have abortions.

Another option is private abortion clinics, which will generally provide the service without hesitation after you have spoken to a counsellor and have shown you really want to end the pregnancy. However, these clinics may not be free in every province.

 Do I need my parents' permission?

Generally speaking, as long as you use the services of a private abortion clinic, you don't need your parents' permission to have an abortion, and you don't need to notify them either. If you go to a hospital, however, there is no standard rule. It depends on the laws in each province or territory and also on the rules of individual hospitals. In British Columbia, for example, there is no age restriction even for abortions performed in public hospitals. In Québec, however, you generally need to be 14 to get an abortion without parental consent, even in a private clinic, as this is the minimum age of consent for medical treatment in that province. Also, no matter where you are, some doctors may encourage teenage patients to discuss their decision with their parents.

Can my parents force me to get an abortion?

Although there is no law against your parents pressuring you to have an abortion, hospitals and clinics are unlikely to perform an abortion on a woman who says she doesn't want one, even if she is a minor. The right to liberty and security of the person guaranteed by section 7 of the Charter of Rights and Freedoms can be interpreted to include the right not only to consent to an abortion but also to refuse one. In the unlikely event that a medical practitioner scheduled an abortion with a parent for a daughter who did not want one, she could contact child protective services. The matter could be taken to court, where a judge could be expected to issue an order preventing the abortion.

Being a Minor Parent

If, after all, a minor gets pregnant, she may choose to keep the child and raise it or to put it up for adoption. The child's father might also have a right to be involved in this decision.[6] However, no one may make this decision for the birth parents. If they choose to put the baby up for adoption, it will legally become the child of someone else, and the birth parents will give up all their legal rights and responsibilities to the adoptive parents.

---

6 A father's rights in this matter are complicated, and they depend on which province or territory you live in. If you want to know what rights you have as the father of your child (or, if you are the mother, what rights your child's father has), we recommend you speak to someone who is an expert in the laws where you live.

Whether they are single, married, or divorced and whether they are living together or apart, if minor parents choose to keep the baby, then according to both common law and a number of provincial statutes, they have the same rights and responsibilities toward their child as do adult parents. At first, this may not seem like such a surprising thing, but, when you think about it, this rule makes the law somewhat inconsistent. There are a great many decisions, some of them relatively trivial, that minors—even those who are fairly mature—cannot make for themselves against the wishes of their parents. Yet if these same minors have their own child, they're suddenly entitled to make all those same decisions for someone else, someone even more vulnerable than themselves, regardless of how mature they are. This inconsistency suggests to us that one reason the law fails to give young people more autonomy in relation to their parents is simply that most adults (the ones who make laws) still believe that parents have a *right* to control their children—not because all minors are necessarily too immature to handle more autonomy.

While becoming a parent does give you certain rights, if you show that you cannot take care of or support your child, or if you abuse it, your child can be put into the care of the state. Although in many cases the parents of minor parents are willing to help their children take care of their own child, they are not generally under an obligation to do so, which would seem to make sense given that they did not choose to have the grandchild.[7] Minor parents have as much of a duty to support their child as do adult parents, and, like any parents, they may lose their child if they cannot or will not fulfill that duty.

In conclusion, sexuality and relationships are an area in which the law restricts your rights in some ways, partly to protect you from exploitation or abuse, yet also gives you greater rights as you get older. You have the option of exercising those rights. At the same time, relationships (especially sexual relationships) aren't all about you. The choices you make affect the lives of other people close to you—not only your partner but also your parents and friends, and potentially your own child. This should motivate you to use your rights responsibly and carefully. Demonstrating responsibility in this very important area of life will also demonstrate your maturity, which will in turn give more weight to the claim that, as a young person, you deserve to be given greater autonomy in other areas as well.

---

7 Article 585 of the Québec Civil Code does say, however, that relatives "in the direct line in the first degree"—that is, parents, offspring, and siblings—owe each other support.

7

CHILD AND FAMILY SERVICES

Although the law gives parents, teachers, and other adults a lot of power over young people, that power has its legal limits. If they cross a certain line, the state has a duty to step in and give you protection. While not everyone agrees on how much power the law should have to intervene in family situations, or on when it should do so and in what way, if government authorities find out that you are not being taken care of properly or are being treated very harshly or abused in some way, they will step in and try to help you.

Like most matters that relate to family law, child welfare (also called child protection) falls under provincial or territorial jurisdiction. Each province or territory has its own child welfare system, so the laws and procedures differ from one place to another. In addition, many Indigenous communities provide child welfare services, although, as a general rule, these services must operate in accordance with provincial or territorial legislation, even if they are based on a First Nations reserve. This is changing, however.

In response to the Truth and Reconciliation Commission's Calls to Action, the federal government recently announced plans to hand over authority for child welfare services to Indigenous governments.[1]

In Canada, child welfare services are provided by government agencies, the names of which vary from one province or territory to another. In Ontario, for example, child welfare is the responsibility of the Ontario Association of Children's Aid Societies, while other jurisdictions use names like "Child Protection Services" or "Child and Family Services" (see the list in appendix C). These agencies employ social workers who are trained in helping children and families cope with difficult problems, including family violence. For the sake of convenience, we will refer to all these various agencies as "social services," and, as an example of legislation, we will use the law of Nova Scotia, where child welfare falls under the Children and Family Services Act.

1 See, for instance, "'No More Scooping Children': Canada, Indigenous Leaders Announce Plan to Co-develop Child Welfare Legislation," *APTN National News*, November 30, 2018, https://aptnnews.ca/2018/11/30/no-more-scooping-children-canada-indigenous-leaders-announce-plan-to-co-develop-child-welfare-legislation/. The TRC was reacting to what has been called a "humanitarian crisis" in Indigenous child welfare, the product of a system widely recognized for its failure to serve the needs of Indigenous children. At present, fewer than 8 percent of all children under 14 in Canada are Indigenous, and yet these children account for more than half of all children in foster care. For more information, see "Indigenous Children and the Child Welfare System in Canada," an overview prepared in September 2017 by the National Collaborating Centre on Aboriginal Health, https://www.ccnsa-nccah.ca/docs/health/FS-ChildWelfareCanada-EN.pdf.

When do social services step in?

The law in Canada mainly cares about protecting young people from two kinds of behaviour, *child abuse* and *child neglect*. Precisely what qualifies as abuse or neglect is a matter of definition, and what some people might consider abusive may not necessarily be what the law views as abusive. As a general rule, though, the law protects youth from the following:

- **Physical abuse:** This occurs when a parent, teacher, or a person who is taking care of a child inflicts (or threatens to inflict) violence on the child, including beating, kicking, and punching the child or using a weapon or dangerous object against him or her, especially if the physical force leaves cuts or bruises or causes more serious injury. As we explained in chapter 3, however, guardians—although not other people—still have the right to inflict mild corporal punishment on their children, within rules laid down by the Supreme Court.

- **Emotional abuse:** This covers a wide range of behaviour that undermines a child's right to feel respected and loved. If parents or caregivers constantly say unkind things to a child or threaten to give the child away to someone else, this is emotional abuse. So is ignoring or not showing any interest in a child, treating a child in a degrading or humiliating way, placing highly unreasonable expectations on a child, or doing any other thing that creates an unhealthy psychological environment for a growing child and thus hinders his or her normal development.

- **Sexual abuse**: This refers to any sexual contact with a child by a parent, teacher, or other person in a position of trust or authority toward the child. This includes not only having sex with a child but also touching the child's body in a sexual way, displaying one's private body parts for a sexual reason, showing a child pornographic images, or using the child to create pornography.

- **Neglect**: A parent or other caregiver who regularly fails to give a child the things that he or she needs in order to grow up safe and healthy is guilty of neglect. Neglect can include not giving the child enough food, clothing, shelter, or medical care; not adequately supervising the child; raising the child in an unhealthy, unhygienic, or dangerous environment; failing to educate the child; not meeting any of the child's emotional needs; not teaching a child to distinguish right from wrong; or not giving him or her sufficient time for rest or exercise.

In some provinces and territories, the law defines child abuse and neglect in greater detail than in others. The terms "child abuse" and "child neglect" may not always be used; instead, the law may speak of a child's being "in need of protection." In Nova Scotia, for example, section 22(2) of the Children and Family Services Act contains a long list of situations in which the law considers a child to be "in need of protective services."

As the above list suggests, the situations in which the law intervenes are usually pretty extreme. A parent may be strict or emotionally somewhat distant, but this does not amount to child abuse, nor is failing to fulfill a child's wants (as opposed to his or her needs) considered neglect. Regardless of what's going on, though, a person can always contact social services, and, at times, social workers may seek to interpret legal definitions rather broadly, so as to enable them to become involved in less extreme situations. Generally speaking, however, they must follow strict rules about when they are allowed to intervene and how. In an emergency situation, they can act quickly, but they will not usually make a serious intervention into a family without a thorough investigation that involves fact-gathering and consultation. In some provinces, once you're 16, social services will step in only if you agree to it.

Anyone can report child abuse or neglect to the police or to social services. In fact, all over Canada, there are laws that require people who know or even suspect that someone is abusing or neglecting a child to report it to the authorities. In Nova Scotia, section 23 of the Children and Family Services Act orders any person "who has information, whether or not it is confidential or privileged, indicating that a child is in need of protective services" to report it immediately. Those who fail to do so can face a fine of up to $2,000 and/or imprisonment for up to six months. Section 24 further specifies that any professional (such as a doctor, teacher, member of the clergy, or youth worker) who has reason to suspect possible child abuse or neglect must immediately contact the authorities or face a fine of up to $5,000 and/or imprisonment for up to a year.

Until what age can social services help me?

Until fairly recently, in quite a few places, the cut-off point for social services was 16. That is, social services would intervene only when an incident involved a child under that age—although once the case was opened, it could remain open even after a young person turned 16 (usually until he or she became a legal adult). At this point, however, in almost every province or territory, social services will take you as a new case until you reach the age of majority. In 2017, Nova Scotia extended most child protection services to all those under 19 (the age of majority in that province), and, at the start of 2018, Ontario adopted a similar policy.

There are just a few exceptions. In Newfoundland and Labrador, if you are 16 or 17, social services will take you as a new case only as long as you are still in high school or an equivalent program; they are also able to intervene if a minor older than 16 has a mental disability or is otherwise not mentally competent to protect himself or herself. In Saskatchewan, social services normally accepts only children under 16 as new cases, but they will do so for 16- or 17-year-olds in circumstances that Child and Family Services considers exceptional. In addition, social services will provide financial and housing assistance, and possibly other protection, to 16- or 17-year-olds whose parents are unwilling to take care of them or who cannot live with their families. In other jurisdictions, even though social services will accept minors aged 16 or over as new cases, the procedures for dealing with youth of that age may differ, as may the services available to them.

In some circumstances, young people who are already in the care of social services can continue to receive help even after they reach the age of majority, especially if they are still studying or are otherwise in the midst of transitioning into adult life. These days, even a young person who was spared abuse or neglect while growing up often needs more time to establish financial independence. For children who were not as lucky, recovering from their childhood can take even longer.

 How can social services help me?

The kind of help that social workers can provide depends on the nature of the problem. In an emergency—if, for example, a child is in physical danger or in need of immediate medical attention—their first priority will be to get the child to a place of safety. Otherwise, they will probably do one or more of the following:

- Talk with a child's parents or guardians, explain what a child needs and why what they are doing is unacceptable, and try to convince them to change their behaviour

- Offer advice to parents or guardians about how to solve problems that relate to their child's upbringing

- Arrange for individual or family counselling

- If a child is too young to be left alone, arrange for a "homemaker"—that is, a person who will come in and take care of the child when there's no one else around

- Recommend that a child be removed from the family home and placed in protective custody (a foster home or group home)

Depending on the situation, a social worker may find other ways to mediate between you and your parents or to offer additional forms of support. What social workers cannot do is force your parents to change their rules, nor can they demand that your parents change their behaviour. However, once social services has become involved, your parents know that they are under scrutiny. If the situation fails to improve—and especially if it deteriorates—social services can have you taken away from your family. The unspoken threat of losing their child is a powerful incentive for many parents to try to do better.

Social workers also cannot punish your parents for anything they do. They can help you get out of a dangerous situation and into a safer place, but they do not have any direct power over adults. Only the police and judges have that, and only in some situations. "Child abuse" and "child neglect" are not, in themselves, federal crimes. In order for those who are guilty of abuse or neglect to be punished, the specific type of abuse or neglect must be a criminal or a provincial offence—injuring or abandoning a child, for example, or not providing the necessaries of life, or not sending a child to school. Child abuse as such may also be a provincial offence, in which case it can carry penalties for the offender within that province. But, while social workers can certainly notify the police and provide evidence in court, they cannot themselves punish someone.

When would I be taken away from my parents?

Young people are sometimes afraid to report abuse and neglect because they don't want to be taken away from their
parents and put into a foster home. As you can see from the
list above, however, removing you from your family home is
only one option, and, except in an emergency situation, it is
usually the last option that social services will consider. In
order to take this action, a social worker does not ordinarily
need your permission (especially if you are under 16), and
it may be that you don't agree with the decision. If social
services does take you into care, however, this is likely to
be only a temporary safety measure, lasting until a judge
either orders that you stay in their care for a longer period
or else decides that you can be returned to your parents. For
example, section 33(4) of Nova Scotia's Children and Family
Services Act states: "Where a child has been taken into care
pursuant to this Section, an agency has the temporary care
and custody of the child until a court orders otherwise or
the child is returned to the parent or guardian."

In addition, while you are living in a foster home or
group home, you will in many cases have the right to
meet with your parents from time to time, and they may
be given a chance to have significant input into raising
you and making decisions about you. Protective custody
is not meant to be permanent: social workers today are
trained to do all they can to help families stay together.
Typically, you will be kept in a foster home only until your
family situation has improved: once the authorities feel

that your parents are able to take proper care of you, you will be returned to your home. (There have, unfortunately, been cases in which a child was returned to a parent who continued to abuse the child afterward. Should this ever happen to you, you should contact social services.) Children usually stay in the permanent care of the state only in extreme situations—if both parents have died, for example, or have committed a serious crime against a child or have shown themselves absolutely unfit or unwilling to take care of their child—and then only if no other relatives are willing or able to take the child in.

For the most part, children are taken into protective custody only when their health, safety, or mental or moral development appears to be at serious risk. All the same, while this is unlikely in the case of relatively minor incidents, the fact is that any time social services is summoned to deal with a situation involving abuse or neglect, there is a chance that they will want to take a child into protective custody—and if you are considering reporting anything to social services, you need to be aware that this could happen. Before making such a decision, however, the social worker will ask lots of questions and proceed very carefully, often consulting with a supervisor. You should also be aware that, regardless of what the social worker decides, your parents could be angry with you for bringing social services into your family situation. They may think that you have no right to imply that they are not good parents or to call their power over you into question. But you should *never* put up with serious abuse or neglect. If you often feel unsafe, unwell, frightened, sad, or hungry, these are good reasons to let the authorities help you.

 How much say do I have in what happens to me?

This depends on your age, as well as on where you live, as provinces and territories have different laws about the age at which the authorities must take the views of a young person into account. In Nova Scotia, section 37 of the Children and Family Services Act says that, if you are 16 or older, you will normally be entitled to have your say in decisions about whether to take you into protective custody, and, if so, where to place you. You can also ask for a lawyer to represent you in court. If you are at least 12 but under 16, you can ask that the court allow you to have a say in the process; if the judge agrees, a litigation guardian will be appointed to represent you. In fact, regardless of a child's age, the court can decide to appoint a litigation guardian, if this appears to be in the child's best interests, or someone else may ask the court to do so.

 Where will I live if I am taken into protective custody?

If you are taken away from your parents, you may be placed with a relative, such as a grandparent, uncle, or aunt. If there is no adult family member who is willing to take care of you and whom the court trusts will do so responsibly, you will be placed either in a foster home—an ordinary household in which adults take care of one or a few young people and try to create a family-like environment—or else in a somewhat larger group home. Old-style orphanages, which housed dozens of abandoned or orphaned children, no longer exist.

If you are to be placed temporarily in foster care, it will be up to social services to decide where you will live. In making this decision, social services will, as far as this is feasible, look for a setting in which you will feel comfortable and welcome. According to section 44(3) of Nova Scotia's Children and Family Services Act, when selecting a foster home or group home, social services is expected to keep several factors in mind: whether it is possible to keep you with your brothers and sisters (if they, too, have been placed in protective care); your need to be able to keep in touch with relatives and friends; your cultural, racial, and linguistic heritage; and your need to be able to continue your education and the practice of your religion. If you are of Indigenous ancestry, the first thing they should consider is a *kinship placement* (that is, placing you with a relative). If this is not possible, they should try to place you with someone from within your community who is an approved foster parent, and, if this isn't possible either, they should try to find an Indigenous foster parent in some other community.

In the event that a court orders a child to be placed in the *permanent* custody of the state, social services will generally look for a foster family that is similar in background to the child's original family. For example, in Nova Scotia, section 47(5) of the Children and Family Services Act orders that such a child "shall be placed with a family of the child's own culture, race, religion or language," provided that one can be found within a reasonable period of time. Failing that, the child is to be placed "in the most suitable home available." In this case, social services will seek a family that will accept and respect the child's cultural differences. Moreover, once children are placed in permanent custody, they are usually available for adoption (a process we discussed in chapter 3).

 What rights do I have in protective custody?

Foster parents are not allowed to treat you in any way they like; they are expected to treat you decently and respect your basic rights. In some provinces (Alberta, British Columbia, Manitoba, Ontario, and Québec), they are forbidden to use any form of corporal punishment, even the relatively mild forms that your actual parents are allowed. In Nova Scotia, a foster home or group home must meet strict fire safety standards and contain an adequate number of rooms and other facilities. You must not be restrained, except as a last resort to control physically aggressive or out-of-control behaviour, and you must be provided with regular meals and all necessary medication (Nova Scotia Regulation 265/2016, sections 23–29). You should also be allowed to practice your religion.[2] At the same time, it is

---

2 According to section 50(1) of the Children and Family Services Act, when a court is called upon to decide whether you are in need of protective services, it must determine what your religion is. Subsection (2) then states that your religion is considered to be the one agreed upon by your parents or guardians but that this is "subject to

your responsibility to behave properly while you are in the home. You are expected to know and obey the rules and to understand that, if you break them, you can be punished in some appropriate fashion.

Either your social worker or the person with whom you are placed should make sure that you understand the rights that children in your province or territory have when they are in protective custody. In Nova Scotia, for example, the law requires that "a child-caring facility must provide the children residing in the facility with written information concerning the facility and the rights and obligations of each child while a resident in the facility" and that this information "must be appropriate to their age and their level of comprehension" (Nova Scotia Regulation 265/2016, ss. 21[1] and 21[2]).[3] They should also explain to you how to make a complaint if the foster parents or the people who run the group home fail to respect your rights. If you have reason to believe that the adults who are supposed to be taking care of you are neglecting or abusing you, you should definitely let your social worker know and file a complaint.

---

the child's views and wishes if they can be reasonably ascertained." In other words, if your own preference clearly differs from that of your parents, your choice may turn out to be decisive. If your religious affiliation is just not clear from what you and your parents have to say, the court can choose to decide which religion, if any, you are considered to belong to.

3 In Nova Scotia, the law doesn't spell out precisely what these rights and obligations should be. In some provinces, however (Ontario, for example), the law goes into greater detail about the rights of children in care.

When you reach the age at which you can withdraw from parental control—which, in many places, is 16 (see table 2)—you can normally leave foster care of your own free will, although, depending on the province, there may be an official procedure that you will have to follow. In addition, some protection orders specify that they can be enforced for longer, most often until you reach the age of majority.

 What if I am still in protective custody when I reach the age of majority?

If you have not been returned to your parents or adopted by the time you become a legal adult, you will have to plan to leave protective custody and be on your own. Depending on the province or territory, it may be possible for you to continue to receive support under certain circumstances, and there may also be services and programs available to help you make the transition to adulthood. In Nova Scotia, section 48(1) of the Children and Family Services Act specifies that an order for permanent care and custody ends when one of four things happen: you reach the age of majority (19, in Nova Scotia); you are adopted; you get married; or an application is made to the court to terminate permanent custody and the court approves it. (The following subsections lay out the terms under which such an application can be made.) If, however, you are disabled, then, when you turn 19, the court can order the care to continue until you turn 21.

Sadly, some parents get away with abusing or neglecting their children for a long time before someone finally notices.

And, even when someone does, child welfare systems are themselves far from perfect. Too often, social services are inadequately funded by provincial or territorial governments, which makes it difficult for them to do their job in the way that they would like. While social workers generally mean well, they may be handling far too many cases, and, despite regulations, foster parents and group homes sometimes break the rules, whether intentionally or unintentionally. Needless to say, we hope that you will never be abused or neglected—especially not to the point that a judge feels it necessary to order you to be placed in protective custody. All the same, in some cases, foster care, even if far from ideal, is a much safer and healthier alternative for youth to staying where they are.

BEING IN CONFLICT WITH THE LAW

As you've probably noticed by now, the law is not only about safeguarding your rights but also about your responsibilities toward others. It obligates you to do certain things, and it prohibits you from doing others. Criminal law sets rules that aim to keep society safe and to ensure that everyone's rights are respected. Breaking one of these rules can carry consequences, for young people as well as for adults, and these consequences can sometimes be serious.

Before we look at what happens when youth break the law, it would be helpful to explain a few things about criminal law in general. In Canada, criminal law falls under federal jurisdiction, according to section 91 of the Constitution Act, 1867. Most criminal offences are defined in the Criminal Code of Canada, which is the main source of criminal law in this country, but several other federal statutes, such as the Controlled Drugs and Substances Act (Canada's main drug control law), name certain crimes. If someone breaks one of these federal rules, that person has committed a criminal offence—that is, a crime.

Yet not all offences against the law are federal crimes. As we explained in the introduction, section 92 of the Constitution Act, 1867 gives provinces and territories the right to make laws in certain areas and to allow municipalities to pass bylaws, provided none of these rules conflict with federal laws. In addition, provinces and territories have the right to enforce these laws, whether by imposing a fine, some other penalty, or even a prison sentence. In this book, we have already encountered many provincial or territorial statutes (concerning, for example, education or child protection), and provinces and territories also enact a great many regulations, such as traffic laws or rules about the use of public lands. While breaking one of these laws is not, strictly speaking, a "crime"—and while many of these provincial and territorial offences are relatively minor—you can be punished for violating them.

In other words, there's more than one way that you can land in trouble with the law. But the most serious way is by committing a criminal offence under federal law.

Criminal Procedure in Brief

When a crime is committed, it is the job of the police and other law enforcement authorities to locate the person believed to be responsible. The offender will then be arrested and charged in court with the offence. If the accused admits that he or she committed the crime, the judge will, after carefully considering the facts of the case, decide on an appropriate *sentence*—that is, a penalty of some sort.

If, instead, the accused claims to be innocent, a trial will take place, during which either a judge alone or a judge and a jury of citizens will try the case. During the trial, they will listen to arguments, first from the Crown and then from the defence.[1] The **Crown attorney** (the government prosecutor) will try to prove that the **defendant** (the accused person) is guilty, and then the defendant—or, more likely, his or her lawyer—will try to show why he or she should be found innocent. In the end, the judge or the jury, if there is one, must reach a **verdict**—a decision one way or the other— about the defendant's guilt. One very important principle is that someone accused of a crime is considered innocent until proven guilty. This means that, if there is any doubt about whether someone is guilty of the crime in question, the person should be found not guilty. If the verdict is "not guilty," the accused is *acquitted* and is free to go. If the verdict is "guilty," the accused is *convicted* of the crime, and the judge will decide on a sentence.

Both the Crown attorney and the defendant are allowed to appeal the verdict—that is, challenge it in a higher court—provided there are legal grounds for doing so. A verdict cannot be challenged simply because either the Crown attorney or the defendant is unhappy with it and

---

1 In Canada, criminal lawsuits are always brought by the Crown—that is, by the state. This is why the names of legal cases so often begin with *R.*, which stands for *Rex* ("King") or *Regina* ("Queen").

would like a higher court to retry the case, in hopes of a different result. A court of appeal will agree to review a lower court's decision if that decision seemed unreasonable, in view of the evidence that was presented, or if it appears that "miscarriage of justice" occurred (for example, if one of the members of the jury was obviously biased). An appeal can also be based on an "error of law" that might have affected the final verdict—if, for instance, the verdict depended on evidence that was not actually admissible in court or if a judge's reasoning was based on a wrong interpretation of a particular law. In the end, the court will either allow or dismiss—that is, accept or reject—the appeal. If the appeal is allowed, then, in most cases, the court will simply order a new trial (although in some cases it might revise the conviction or even acquit the accused).

Types of Crimes

According to section 718.1 of the Criminal Code, "A sentence must be proportionate to the gravity of the offence and the degree of responsibility of the offender." So, when it comes to sentencing, the Criminal Code usually specifies a range of options for particular offences, such as a fine of *no more than* a certain amount and/or a jail term of *up to* a certain number of years. While the specific options vary depending on the offence, in general terms, a sentence reflects the kind of crime that was committed. The Criminal Code divides crimes into three broad groups:

- *Indictable offences*: These are serious crimes, such as murder, manslaughter, robbery, treason, or acts of terrorism. Punishments can be very serious for **indictable offences**. In Canada, the harshest punishment—for crimes such as first-degree murder—is life imprisonment with no chance of **parole** (an early release, on certain conditions) for twenty-five years. If there is reason to believe that a criminal might pose a long-term danger to society, he or she may be declared a "dangerous offender," in which case he or she could be sentenced to remain in prison for an unspecified period (perhaps even life).

- *Summary offences*: These are relatively minor crimes. An example is public nudity (Criminal Code, s. 174). There are certainly exceptions, but **summary offences** usually carry a punishment of no more than six months in jail, a maximum fine of $5,000, or both.

- *Hybrid offences*: These are crimes that can be tried either as indictable offences or as summary offences, depending on the choice of the prosecution (that is, the Crown). In making the decision, the prosecution will consider several factors, such as how serious the offence committed was and whether the offender has committed crimes in the past. Most of the crimes in the Criminal Code are hybrid offences; examples include assault with a weapon, possession of cocaine, and fraud involving less than $5,000. The penalty will depend on which way the offence is tried.

As we will see below, young offenders are generally given milder sentences than adults. In fact, even though much of the Criminal Code applies to youth as well as to adults, Canada (like many other countries) has a separate system for dealing with young people who commit crimes.

Youth Criminal Justice

In Canada, the Youth Criminal Justice Act (YCJA) is the main law that lays down the rules about what happens to young offenders. It was passed in 2003, to replace the Young Offenders Act, which itself replaced an even earlier law, the Juvenile Delinquents Act. Like its predecessors, the Youth Criminal Justice Act tries to strike a balance between two responses to youth crime that pull the law in different directions. On the one hand, because young people don't have as much experience as adults, their judgment may be imperfect, and so it would be wrong to punish them as harshly as adults. On the other hand, young people do need to learn to take responsibility for their actions, so it would be wrong not to punish them at all.

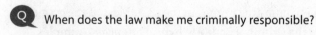 When does the law make me criminally responsible?

In Canada today, the age of criminal responsibility is 12—higher than in some countries, and lower than in others. If someone under 12 commits a crime, he or she cannot be charged with it. He or she will not be put on trial and so cannot be found guilty (Criminal Code, s. 13).

FACT FILE   The Evolution of Youth Criminal Justice
in Canada

The way that criminal law treats youth has changed a
great deal over the years. In colonial times, children as
young as 7 were held criminally responsible for their
actions. There was no separate system of youth justice: if a child committed a crime, the same sentence
could be imposed as would be on an adult—including,
in theory, the death penalty. Once the Criminal Code
was enacted, in 1892, some effort was made to distinguish between young offenders and adults, but the
first major change came with the Juvenile Delinquents
Act of 1908. Whereas previously the focus had fallen
on punishment, the new act adopted a child welfare
approach, according to which a young offender should
be treated "not as a criminal, but as a misdirected and
misguided child, and one needing aid, encouragement,
help and assistance" (7–8 Edward 7, c. 40, s. 31). The
act made the young offender guilty of "delinquency,"
rather than of the specific crime that he or she had
committed. It also discouraged putting children under
the age of 12 into correctional institutions until efforts
had been made to reform the child in his or her own
home or in a foster home or through the intervention of a children's aid society. In addition, it required
parents to assume some measure of responsibility for
their child's behaviour.

On the down side, the Juvenile Delinquents
Act allowed judges to sentence young offenders in
whatever way they thought best. A youth might be

placed in foster care or be locked up in a reformatory or a juvenile detention facility for an indefinite period of time, possibly until the youth turned 21. The same fate could befall a young person who had not actually committed a crime but had simply done something that adults didn't like (such as running away from home or being sexually active). Such a youth could be charged with a "status offence"—an action that becomes an offence only when the person doing it is underage. A similar approach was evident in provincial laws that allowed a child who was constantly getting into trouble to be declared "incorrigible"—that is, incapable of learning to behave properly—and placed in an institution, again perhaps indefinitely. Parents sometimes even accused their own children of being incorrigible simply in order to have them taken off their hands. Such laws were repealed long ago, but they're a good reminder of how far things have come.

In 1984, the Juvenile Delinquents Act was replaced by the Young Offenders Act. The new law raised the age of criminal responsibility to 12, and it also eliminated status offences and the general charge of "delinquency." Instead, a young offender had to be charged with a specific crime. Unless the case was tried in an adult court (which was possible if the offender was at least 14 and mandatory if he or she had committed a very serious crime), the most severe sentence an offender under the age of 18 could receive was three years' imprisonment. The idea was that young people should be held responsible for their actions but not to the same degree as adults.

However, many people felt that the Young Offenders Act was too lenient, and the act was eventually amended to provide for longer terms of imprisonment. In contrast, others complained that the rate at which Canadian youth were sent to prison was significantly higher than the rate in other countries and that the act was therefore too harsh.

In 2003, the law's treatment of young offenders was reformed again, when the Young Offenders Act was replaced by the Youth Criminal Justice Act. While retaining the idea that youth should be held accountable for their behaviour but not to the same extent as adults, this law lays greater stress on alternative forms of punishment that aim to keep youth out of the court process, as well as on the reintegration of youthful offenders into the community. It also requires that, if a young person does have to be placed on trial, the case must be heard in a youth court—although, in some circumstances, the youth can be given the same sentence as an adult.

A minimum age of 12 doesn't mean that, if you commit a crime before you reach that age, nothing will happen. Chances are that your parents will punish you, and, depending on what you did, you might also be disciplined by your school or, for example, banned from a store in which you were caught shoplifting. In addition, social services could become involved, especially if you have committed a fairly serious crime. Criminal behaviour is very often a symptom of other problems, often having to do with psychological or emotional adjustment. So when a child does something seriously wrong, this could be a signal of problems in the child's home environment or possibly evidence of a developmental disorder. If nothing else, such behaviour calls for a response of some sort.

This concern about the reasons that children commit crimes is reflected in certain provincial laws. For example, section 74(2) of Ontario's Child, Youth and Family Services Act, 2017 contains a list of circumstances under which a child is considered to be "in need of protection." Clause (l) deals with situations in which a child under 12 "has killed or seriously injured another person or caused serious damage to another person's property" and "services or treatment are necessary to prevent a recurrence." If, in such circumstances, the child's parents or guardians fail to make arrangements for the necessary services or treatment (such as a psychiatric evaluation and possible counselling), the child is deemed to be in need of protection. As clause (m) goes on to say, a child under 12 is also in need of protection if he or she "has on more than one occasion injured another person or caused loss or damage to another person's property," either "with the encouragement of the person having charge of the child or because of that person's failure or inability to supervise the child adequately." As we saw in the previous chapter, a child in need of protection can be taken into protective custody, placed in a foster home, and given the care that social services consider necessary under the circumstances.

The Youth Criminal Justice Act defines a "young person" as someone aged 12 to 17. In other words, once you turn 12, you can be arrested and charged with a crime, and you will be dealt with in accordance with the rules and procedures laid out in the act. Once you turn 18, however, you are, in the eyes of the criminal law, an adult, even in parts of Canada where the age of majority is actually 19.

Getting Arrested

According to section 495 of the Criminal Code, the police can arrest you if you are caught in the act of committing a criminal offence or if a police officer has reason to believe that you have committed an indictable offence or that you are about to do so.[2] If, however, the crime of which you are suspected is *not* an indictable offence under federal law, then, in order to arrest you, the police must first obtain a **warrant** (that is, a court document ordering that you be arrested)—unless the officer has reasonable grounds to believe that a warrant already exists for your arrest.

---

2 It might seem strange that the police are allowed to arrest someone who hasn't actually committed a crime. But the purpose of such arrests is to prevent crime, rather than to punish people. According to section 503(4) of the Criminal Code, when the police arrest someone whom they believe is about to commit a crime, they must release the person unconditionally as soon as they are satisfied that "the continued detention of that person in custody is no longer necessary in order to prevent the commission by him [or her] of an indictable offence"—that is, as soon as they feel sure that, once released, the person isn't going to go ahead and commit the crime anyway.

The police do not necessarily have to arrest a suspect. If they feel that an offence is too minor to be worth prosecuting, they can choose to take no further action, or they may let the culprit off with a milder penalty, such as a verbal warning or a more formal "caution" or "referral." (These penalties are examples of "extrajudicial measures," which we'll discuss in more detail below.) There is absolutely no guarantee of this, however: if an offence has been committed, the police have the right to pursue prosecution.

 What happens if I'm arrested?

When someone is arrested, the person is typically restrained by the police, handcuffed, and informed that he or she is under arrest. The suspect must then be told why he or she is being arrested (that is, what offence he or she is charged with) and that he or she has the right to consult with a lawyer. These basic rights are protected under section 10 of the Charter of Rights and Freedoms, according to which anyone who is arrested or detained has the right "to be informed promptly of the reasons therefor" and "to retain and instruct counsel without delay and to be informed of that right." In addition, according to paragraph 146(2)(b) of the Youth Criminal Justice Act, young offenders must also be informed that they have the right to call their parents or, if no parent is available, another adult who could help them, and they must also be told that anything they say could be used in court as evidence against them. All this information must be given to you in language that you can readily understand.

If you are arrested and charged with a crime, one of two things will happen, depending on the seriousness of the offence:

- You may be taken to the police station and then released. In this case, you will be given an "appearance notice" ordering you to appear in court on a particular day for an initial hearing.

- You may be taken to the police station, where you will be booked—that is, your identity, the time of your arrest, and the reasons for your arrest will be recorded. Then you will be put in a cell. If this happens, you cannot be held for longer than twenty-four hours before being brought before a judge for a bail hearing (as we'll describe below).

 If I'm arrested, do the police have to tell my parents?

Yes. As soon as is reasonably possible, the police must inform the parents of a youth who has been arrested and detained. If they can't locate at least one parent, they must inform an adult relative or other adult known to the youth who may be able to provide assistance. Also, if you've been given an appearance notice, the police must see to it that your parents (or other adult) receive a written copy of this notice. All this is spelled out in section 26 of the Youth Criminal Justice Act.

Will the police ask me questions?

Probably so—but apart from giving them your name, age, and address, you have the right not to tell them anything. As we noted above, prior to questioning you, the police have to let you know that any information you provide voluntarily can be used as evidence against you in court—but this includes any statements you make spontaneously at the time of your arrest, before the police have had time to inform you of your rights (YCJA, s. 146[3]). They must also tell you that you have the right to consult with a lawyer and then give you a reasonable opportunity to do so. However, the police may ask you to "waive" (that is, give up) your right to consult with a lawyer before answering questions; we strongly advise you not to do this. You should know that, when arresting a suspect, the police sometimes use quite aggressive methods in an effort to persuade the person to admit his or her guilt at the outset or to provide information that the police would like to have. Although the police are not supposed to do anything that is actually against the law, there have been cases where the police have used threats or even physical force in order to try to get someone to confess. Paragraph 146(2)(b) of the Youth Criminal Justice Act specifies that you have a right to have a lawyer present during questioning. If you waive your right to counsel, however, you no longer have this protection.

Q Do I need a lawyer?

We would say that you do. As mentioned above, at the time of your arrest, the police must inform you that you have the right to contact a lawyer (or, as the case may be, to ask your parents or some other adult to do so for you). You also have the right to be represented by a lawyer in court. If you or your family cannot pay for a lawyer, then, at your initial hearing, the court will either refer you to a legal aid program, if one exists in the province or territory in which you were arrested, or else, on your request, will put you in touch with a court-appointed lawyer (YCJA, s. 25).

If you are charged with a crime, it is very important that you have a lawyer, as he or she will understand court procedure and will know how best to defend you, as well as what steps you need to take at different points during the trial. Being charged with a crime carries serious consequences, and you need expert guidance to avoid pitfalls. Moreover, a lawyer can help you if you feel that the police were overly aggressive at the time of your arrest. According to section 24(2) of the Charter of Rights and Freedoms, if the evidence against you was obtained in a way that violated your rights (if, for example, the police stopped you on the street and searched you without a warrant), then that evidence is not "admissible" in court—that is, it cannot be used. In addition, section 146 of the Youth Criminal Justice Act lays out specific rules concerning the admissibility of evidence obtained from a young person who has been arrested. A lawyer will know all these rules and how they might be used to help you.

Although section 25(7) of the Youth Criminal Justice Act allows you to be represented by a responsible adult such as a parent, other family member, or friend, rather than by a lawyer, we do not recommend this. Unlike a lawyer, these adults will probably not have much familiarity with the law and with court procedure, nor will they necessarily understand the various options that the youth criminal justice system offers. Moreover, their emotional attachment to you as their child or family member may affect their judgment and make it hard for them to think like a lawyer when defending you, which could work to your disadvantage in the long run. Everyone who is charged with a crime should have a lawyer to defend them. There is simply no good reason not to request one.

 Can I be released on bail, or will I be locked up?

As we mentioned above, if you are arrested and charged, you will either be given an appearance notice and released or else you will be detained until your bail hearing. In most cases, it's the first, but there are some exceptions. According to section 497(1.1) of the Criminal Code (which applies to youth as well as adults), the police may detain you if they need to identify you (for example, if you refuse to give them your name), if they need you in order to preserve evidence relating to the offence, or if they think that, were you to be released, you might commit another offence or pose a danger to someone. They can also choose to detain you if they have reason to believe that, if they let you go, you would subsequently fail to show up in court on the appointed date.

If you are detained at the time of your arrest, a bail hearing must take place within twenty-four hours. At this hearing, the court will decide whether you can be released while you await your trial or whether you should remain in custody. The Crown attorney may argue that you should not be released on bail, in which case he or she will attempt to convince the judge that, if you are released, you are likely to commit another crime or that you will run away and not show up for your trial. In response, your lawyer will try to convince the judge that it is, in fact, safe to release you on bail.

If the judge allows you to be released, you will be given a "bail form" to sign in which you promise to appear in court on the date of your trial. The judge may attach a list of certain conditions to your bail. These could include:

- that you or another person agree to pay a certain sum of money if you fail to appear for your trial;

- that you stay with your parents or another responsible person and obey their rules;

- that you stay away from certain people and/or places (usually ones that have some connection to your crime);

- that you refrain from drinking alcohol and using recreational drugs;

- that you attend school or show up for work; and/or

- that you remain where you are and not do any travelling.

If instead you are denied bail, then there must be a good reason for keeping you in custody prior to your trial. Section 29(2) of the Youth Criminal Justice Act specifies that you cannot be kept in detention unless you have been accused of a serious offence or else have a history of criminal behaviour. In addition, according to section 29(1), a judge cannot order the detention of a youth as a substitute for appropriate child protection, mental health treatment, or other social measures. In other words, you can't be locked up for reasons that are not directly related to the crime of which you are accused.

Moreover, even if a youth could legally be kept in detention, a judge *may* choose to release the young person into the custody of a responsible adult (who could be a parent), provided the person "is willing and able to take care of and exercise control over the young person" and make sure that he or she appears in court on the scheduled date and provided the young person agrees to this arrangement (YCJA, s. 31). But a judge is not obliged to do this.

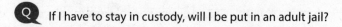 If I have to stay in custody, will I be put in an adult jail?

Section 30(3) of the Youth Criminal Justice Act states that a young person must be detained separately from adult prisoners. This makes good sense: a young offender should not be locked up with hardened criminals, who could have a corrupting influence and might even be dangerous. However, there is no guarantee that, if you must remain in custody, you will be placed in a facility designed specifically for young people. If no youth facility is available within a reasonable distance, you may be placed in an adult facility (although you should be housed separately from adults). A judge may also decide that, for reasons of your own safety or the safety of others, it would be best not to place you in a youth facility. In addition, as section 30(4) specifies, if you turn 18 while you are waiting for your case to be heard, a "provincial director" (an official responsible for administering the Youth Criminal Justice Act) can apply to the youth justice court to have you transferred to a correctional facility for adults.[3] If this happens, then the court is required to hear your opinion before making a decision about the transfer.

If you do end up in detention, remember that you have certain rights in custody, such as the right to decent living conditions, the right not to be physically punished or otherwise mistreated, and, as mentioned above, the right to be separated from adult offenders. You also have the right to a reasonably speedy trial. If at any point you think that your rights are being violated, you should contact your lawyer.

---

3 Most jurisdictions have several "provincial directors," who are appointed by the provincial or territorial government. While they have various duties, they are frequently involved with the supervision of youth who are in trouble with the law.

Extrajudicial Measures

The Youth Criminal Justice Act allows the police or the Crown attorney an alternative to putting a young person on trial. Whenever possible, they are encouraged to offer a young offender "extrajudicial" measures, that is, penalties that do not involve the court system. As section 4 of the act indicates, especially when the offence in question did not involve violence, extrajudicial measures should be preferred as long as the police or the Crown attorney feel satisfied that such measures are adequate to hold a young person accountable for his or her actions. This approach spares a young person from having to be placed on trial and risking a conviction, a sentence, and a youth criminal record. (We'll explain about criminal records later on.) In laying out this option, the act includes some of the principles of *restorative justice*, an approach that emphasizes the rehabilitation of offenders, as opposed to their punishment. Restorative justice stresses the need for offenders to acknowledge the harm they have caused, not only to their victim but to the community as a whole, and to take steps to mend broken relationships.[4]

---

4 If you are interested in learning more about restorative justice, you could begin with the "Restorative Justice" page on the website of the Office of the Federal Ombudsman for Victims of Crime, https://www.victimsfirst.gc.ca/res/pub/gfo-ore/RJ.html. As the page notes, restorative justice approaches owe much to Indigenous legal systems. A good introduction to this subject is *Returning to the Teachings: Exploring Aboriginal Justice*, by Rupert Ross (Toronto: Penguin Books, 1996; new ed., 2006).

The Youth Criminal Justice Act distinguishes two levels of extrajudicial measures. The first consists of warnings, cautions, and referrals, all of which are actions usually taken by the police. Whereas a warning is most often issued verbally, a "caution" (which can also come from the Crown attorney) is a more formal procedure and may include a letter from the police to your parents. In accordance with section 6(1), the police also have the option of a "referral"—that is, sending you to a community-based program or agency that helps youth learn to avoid crime, provided that you agree to this plan.

If these measures don't seem adequate, another possible alternative to prosecution is a "sanction." Extrajudicial sanctions (described in section 10 of the YCJA) are an option if the police or the Crown attorney thinks that such an approach would serve both your own needs and the interests of society. However, you must freely consent to the sanction, and you must also accept responsibility for the action that forms the basis of the offence of which you are accused.[5] Sanctions cannot be used if you deny that you were involved in committing the offence or if you would prefer that the matter be dealt with in court.

Some of the more common sanctions are:

• performing a useful service in the community

---

5 Accepting responsibility for this action is *not* the equivalent of a "guilty" plea. As section 10(4) of the Youth Criminal Justice Act makes clear, if you are ultimately placed on trial for the offence, your admission of responsibility for this action will not be considered admissible evidence. That is, it cannot be used against you later on.

- paying the victim for the damage you have caused
- writing a letter of apology to the victim
- participating in mediation with the victim
- participating in a remedial workshop

One possible problem is that, to be an option, sanctions must be part of a formal program of sanctions authorized for use in your province or territory. Moreover, whether this program is actually available in your community depends on the existence of a local youth justice committee. These committees, which are made up of community residents, help to administer the Youth Criminal Justice Act. Their work includes setting up programs or services for young offenders, facilitating mediation between an offender and the victim, and enlisting community support for extrajudicial approaches to youth crime. Unfortunately, though, such committees don't exist everywhere.

Once you do whatever the extrajudicial sanction requires of you, you are free from further responsibility under the law. If, however, you do not fulfill these obligations on time and as agreed, the Crown attorney may bring your case back to the youth justice court for a new hearing. In that situation, what happens will depend on whether the court feels that, under the circumstances, you've done a good enough job of completing the task you were set. If the court is not satisfied with your efforts to fulfill your responsibilities, it may order that you be placed on trial for the offence with which you've been charged.

If you participate in extrajudicial measures, your parents will be informed, and the victim of your crime will also be given your name as well as information about what measures were taken, if he or she asks to know (YCJA, ss. 10 and 11). Although there will be a record of your participation in extrajudicial measures, this record will be closed after two years.

Going to Court and Giving Evidence

Even though the Youth Criminal Justice Act does encourage measures designed to keep young people out of the judicial system, if you are charged with a crime, you may end up having to go to court, especially if you've committed a relatively serious offence and/or have a history of criminal behaviour. As you probably know, a courtroom is a very solemn and formal environment. It is necessary to be on your best behaviour at all times, to speak to the judge respectfully, and not to talk unless you are asked a question. Your lawyer will know how and when to speak on your behalf. You should wear clean, inoffensive clothes and avoid chewing gum. Also, headgear is not allowed in a courtroom unless it is worn for religious reasons.

According to section 14(1) of the Youth Criminal Justice Act, a young person must be tried in a youth court (as opposed to an adult court) for any offence committed before he or she turned 18. It doesn't matter whether you have withdrawn from parental control or have gotten married:

what counts here is your age. A youth court is much the same as an adult court, except that the press is not allowed inside and trials are normally conducted by a judge alone, without a jury. Only a youth accused of murder or one for whom an adult sentence is sought may choose whether to be tried by a judge and jury or simply by a judge alone. Were you to find yourself in this situation, we would urge you to talk with your lawyer before making the choice: he or she will be able to advise you about which option is more likely to work to your advantage.

As mentioned above, when you are placed on trial, you will be asked in court whether you plead guilty or not guilty. If you are innocent, you should *never* plead guilty, since otherwise you will face punishment for something you have not done. Even if you know, or at least suspect, that you are guilty of the crime in question, you should always consult with your lawyer before entering a guilty plea. Also, according to paragraph 11(c) of the Charter of Rights and Freedoms, you cannot be forced to testify (that is, give evidence) at a trial in which *you* are the person accused, although nothing prohibits you from doing so. Whether it makes sense for you to testify depends on the case and is something else that you should discuss with your lawyer.

However, if you saw a crime being committed or were a victim of one, you may very well be called to testify at the trial of the person accused of the crime. In that case, you will receive a **subpoena**, a letter saying that you must come to court on a certain date to give your evidence. (If you fail to appear on the date specified, the police can get orders to arrest you and bring you to court.) At the trial, both the Crown attorney and the accused's lawyer will ask you questions about what happened during the crime and about what you were doing there—that is, how you came to witness the events. They may ask very detailed questions, so, before you appear in court, try to remember as much as possible and make notes for yourself about what happened. Before you give your evidence, you will be asked to swear an oath to tell the truth, the whole truth, and nothing but the truth. If you don't know the answer to a question that you are asked, you can simply say so—but if you lie while you are giving evidence, you commit a crime called *perjury*. This is a serious offence, punishable by up to 14 years in prison.

Testifying against someone can be scary, especially if you fear that the accused person may be angry and try to harm you in some way to take revenge. But it is your duty to give evidence. Refusing to do so makes you guilty of the crime called *contempt of court*, which, while not as serious as perjury, is punishable by up to 90 days in prison, a fine of $100, or both. Fortunately, according to section 13 of the Charter, evidence you give against someone else cannot subsequently be used against you in a different trial in which *you* are the one accused (unless you are on trial for perjury or for giving conflicting evidence).

Youth Sentences

If you are found guilty of an offence, you will probably receive a youth sentence. (In some circumstances, youth can be given adult sentences: we'll explain about this in the next section.) In choosing a sentence, judges must abide by certain principles, which are laid out in section 38 of the Youth Criminal Justice Act. The basic goal of youth sentencing is to rehabilitate young offenders—that is, to teach them a sense of responsibility for their actions and to help them learn to respect the rights of other people, so that they won't continue to commit crimes. As a general rule, a judge must select the least severe sentence that seems capable of achieving this goal. In so doing, the judge must consider a number of different factors, including the nature of the offence, what prompted the young person to commit it, and whether he or she has a history of convictions.

The various possible youth sentences are listed in section 42(2) of the Youth Criminal Justice Act. While youth sentences are typically more lenient than adult sentences (and cannot be harsher than adult ones), some are more lenient than others. If a judge thinks that a relatively mild punishment will be enough to serve the basic goal of sentencing, your sentence is likely to consist of one or more of the following:

- A formal reprimand from the judge

- An absolute discharge. This means that, even though you have been found guilty, the judge decides not to punish you, and you are free to go. This decision has the effect of undoing your conviction, so you won't have a criminal record. Although judges don't hand out absolute discharges lightly, this could happen if you had been put on trial for a relatively minor offence and, in the opinion of the judge, a conviction would not be in your best interests and your release would not pose any danger to society.

- A conditional discharge. Unlike an absolute discharge, a conditional discharge is accompanied by an order requiring you to abide by certain conditions for a period of time. Again, because this is a discharge, you will not be convicted—unless you violate the conditions, in which case you will have to return to court for further sentencing.

- A fine, which cannot exceed $1,000

- An order to pay compensation to the person you have harmed or to return or replace property that you have stolen or damaged

- An order to perform a service for the person you have harmed. Performing this service cannot take more than 240 hours, nor can it overlap with your school or work hours, and it must be completed within twelve months.

- An order to perform a community service, such as helping out at a hospital, a nursing home, or a municipal department. In this case, you will be given a say in what kind of service you are assigned. Again, performing this service cannot interfere with your school or work hours, and it cannot exceed 240 hours over a period of a year.

- A prohibition order. Such an order prohibits you from possessing something connected to your crime—including, but not limited to, weapons or explosives—for a period of time. For some crimes, you *must* receive a prohibition order, and, in this case, it will apply for at least two years. (If you go to jail as well, the period of the prohibition order starts when you are released.)

A judge is free to impose some combination of these sentences, such as a fine and an order to perform community service. As you may have noticed, some of these punishments are not very different from extrajudicial sanctions. So, even if you are tried in court for your offence, your punishment might not be all that different—although, if you are found guilty and convicted, you will have a youth criminal record.

If, instead, a judge feels that one or more of the above measures will not be sufficient to hold you accountable for your crime and prevent you from committing further offences, he or she can choose to impose a heavier sentence. These penalties fall into two basic categories:

Probation. If you are put on probation, you will not be imprisoned, but for a period of time you will be supervised by the court. You will also be given a probation order specifying certain conditions that you must obey. At a minimum, you will be required not to get into any further trouble and to appear in court if and when requested (YCJA, s. 55[1]). In all likelihood, however, the judge will impose additional conditions. For example, a judge may require you to attend school or to find some form of employment; to remain within your province or territory; to notify the court if you change your address, your school, or your place of work; to live with your parents or another responsible adult and obey their house rules; and/or to not possess a weapon. In addition, a judge can impose any other conditions that he or she feels will promote good behaviour and help to prevent you from committing further offences (YCJA, s. 55[2]). So, for instance, a judge might order you not to associate with certain people or hang out in certain places or to avoid drinking alcohol or using drugs (except for medical reasons).[6]

A probation order requires your signature; before signing it, you should go over the conditions it imposes with your lawyer and make sure you understand them. Although a conditional discharge also comes with an order obliging you to adhere to certain conditions, probation differs in two important ways. First, it is *not* a discharge: it is a sentence that comes with a conviction. And, second, it entails considerably closer supervision. If you receive a conditional discharge, you might be ordered to check in periodically with an official (a "provincial director") who works with the youth justice system. In the case of probation, however,

---

6 As we saw earlier, at an initial bail hearing, a judge may choose to impose similar conditions on your temporary release. If you are subsequently put on probation, the judge may decide to extend some or all of these conditions and/or to impose new ones.

a judge can assign you to a probation officer, who will monitor your behaviour and with whom you must meet on a regular basis.

Probation can last for up to two years, or up to three years if you have been found guilty of more than one crime. If you run into a problem that makes it hard for you to abide by the conditions of the probation order, you can ask the judge to change them (although you need a really good reason to make such a request). If you *violate* the conditions of probation, however, you commit an offence and may be punished for it as well as for your original offence.

Custody. If you have committed a violent offence or if you have committed a serious one and have a history of criminal behaviour or if you have failed to comply with the terms of a lesser sentence, a judge can issue a *custody and supervision order*. This sentence requires you to spend a specified period of time in a youth custody facility (that is, a jail for young people), followed by a period of "conditional supervision" within the community. As is clear from section 39 of the Youth Criminal Justice Act, a custody and supervision order is a sentence of last resort. A judge can issue such an order only if the court has carefully considered all the possible alternatives and is convinced that no other reasonable option exists. One such option is a *deferred custody and supervision order*, which a judge can issue if the offence you committed did not involve physical violence. In this case, you will *not* be put in jail if, during a period of up to six months, you are on good behaviour and abide by certain conditions, which will be spelled out in the order (see YCJA, ss. 105[2] and [3]). While these conditions are very similar to those that might appear in a probation order, if you break them, you could well end up in jail.

As we explained earlier, if you are sentenced to a term in jail and a youth facility is not available in your area, you can be placed in an adult jail, although you should be separated from adult offenders. A provincial director will decide whether you should be placed in a maximum security facility or whether less strict supervision would be enough. In making this decision, he or she must consider factors such as the seriousness of your crime, the likelihood that you will attempt to escape, the safety of the people with whom you are to be imprisoned, and your personal needs.

Unless you have committed a very serious offence (such as manslaughter or attempted murder), the total period you spend in custody and under supervision cannot be longer than two years, with two-thirds of that time being spent in custody and one-third under supervision. If, however, you are convicted of an offence for which an adult could be sentenced to life imprisonment, the total period can be extended to three years, of which two years would be spent in custody and one would be under supervision. Similarly, if you have committed more than one crime for which you are sentenced separately, the combined time of these sentences cannot usually exceed three years. But for first-degree murder, you can get up to ten years (with up to six in custody and four under supervision), and, for second-degree murder, you can get up to seven years (with up to four in custody and three under supervision.) In all these cases, the prosecution can ask the judge to require you to remain in custody for a longer period or even for the whole sentence, which could happen if there is reason to believe that there are things that make you violent and a threat to the community. Very serious offenders who have mental health issues may be sentenced to a special treatment program called "intensive rehabilitative custody."

While you are in custody, your sentence must be reviewed by the youth court once a year. However, at any point, a provincial director can request that such a review be conducted, provided there are sufficient grounds for doing so (see YCJA, s. 94[6]), and you or your parents can also ask a provincial director to make such a request. It is therefore possible (although by no means guaranteed) that the period you must spend in custody could be shortened. After you are released from custody, you will spend the remainder of your sentence under supervision. During this period, you will be required to report in periodically to a provincial director and to abide by certain conditions, much like those in a probation order.

Q What if I'm convicted of a provincial offence not in the Criminal Code?

As a general rule, provincial (or territorial) offences are not as serious as federal crimes and tend to carry lesser penalties, typically fines, but sometimes also briefer periods of imprisonment in a correctional facility. Such convictions do not produce a criminal record, although the local police can choose to keep a record of them for certain purposes. There is no standard way in which provinces and territories treat young people, as opposed to adults, although Ontario's Provincial Offences Act lays out some special provisions for youth over 12 but under 16. For example, according to section 97(1), if a youth is found guilty of a provincial offence, a judge may impose the same fine as for an adult, or the maximum fine for the offence, or a fine of $300, whichever is the least. Alternatively, the judge can put the young person on probation or else decide not to convict him or her at all and issue an absolute discharge. In addition, section 101(1) specifies that a youth cannot be imprisoned (except possibly for violating a probation order, and then for no more than thirty days) or fined more than $1,000.

Adult Sentences

If you are charged with an offence that you committed when you were at least 14 years old (provinces may choose to raise this age to 15 or 16) and for which an adult could be sentenced to more than two years in jail, the prosecution can make an application to the youth court to have you given an adult sentence if you are found guilty. In fact, if your crime was a serious violent offence, the prosecution *must* consider asking for an adult sentence, and if they decide not to do so, they must explain to the court why they chose not to. If the prosecution wishes to seek an adult sentence, you must be informed of this before you enter a plea or before the trial begins (see YCJA, s. 64). You must also be allowed to choose whether you want to be tried by a youth court judge without a jury *and* without a preliminary inquiry, or just by a judge without a jury, or by a judge and a jury (s. 67).[7] You should discuss these options with your lawyer before making the choice.

Before the judge decides whether an adult sentence is appropriate, there must be a hearing at which you, your lawyer, and your parents can argue that you deserve a youth sentence (see YCJA, ss. 71 and 72). The fundamental assumption underlying the youth justice system is that, although young people do need to be held accountable for their behaviour, they are not yet mature enough to be able to fully comprehend the consequences of their actions and clearly distinguish right from wrong. So, before making a final decision about an adult sentence, the judge must consider whether this assumption still applies to you. At the hearing, it will be up to the prosecution to convince the judge that you actually *did* understand that what you were doing was wrong and that a relatively brief youth sentence would not be enough to hold you accountable for your crime. If the prosecution is successful, and the judge does decide to impose an adult sentence, you can appeal the decision.

---

7 The rules governing preliminary inquiries are set out in Part XVIII of the Criminal Code. The purpose of such an inquiry is to determine whether the prosecution actually has enough evidence to bring the accused person to trial. At the end of the inquiry, the judge will either order the defendant to stand trial or else issue a discharge.

If you are given an adult sentence, you will receive the same punishment that an adult would get under the Criminal Code, and the same conditions for parole will apply to your sentence. You can also be sent to an adult jail, such as a federal penitentiary, although it is more likely that you will be held at a youth facility until you turn 18 (and perhaps even longer, if the judge considers this to be in your best interests: your lawyer may be able to make a case for keeping you in a youth facility). Moreover, whereas the names of youth who are convicted of crimes cannot be made public, you lose this protection of your privacy if you are sentenced as an adult, and you will also have an adult criminal record.

Criminal Records

A criminal record is one of the many consequences of being convicted of a crime. These records are kept in a database by the RCMP and are available to the police and the government. Perhaps the biggest disadvantage of a criminal record (especially for an adult) is that many employers and other organizations ask job candidates or prospective volunteers to agree to a criminal record check—and if this check shows that the person has been convicted of a crime, the applicant will probably not be hired or even be allowed to volunteer. Not only can this make it very difficult for people who have served time in jail to find a job, but it also frustrates their efforts to become part of mainstream society again.

The good news for people who have an adult criminal record is that, after a certain period of time, it may be possible to seal the record. The Parole Board of Canada (PBC) grants "record suspensions" to people who can prove that they have become good citizens after serving their sentence. If you have an adult criminal record, you can apply to the PBC for a record suspension five years after completing a sentence for a summary offence or ten years after completing a sentence for an indictable offence. (Some very serious offences, however, such as sexual crimes involving a child, are usually not eligible for a record suspension.) If granted, a record suspension does not erase a criminal record, but it causes it to be separated from the main database, after which it will not normally appear on criminal record checks.

 If I don't get an adult sentence, will I still have a criminal record?

Yes, but youth criminal records are a little different. Unlike an adult record, a youth record does not usually stay open permanently—although there is a misconception that a youth record is automatically erased when you turn 18. Although a youth record is not open forever, the rules are more complex. They are set out mainly in section 119(2) of the YCJA and include the following main points:

- If you are found not guilty, your record will be closed two months after the end of the appeal period (assuming the Crown does not appeal your acquittal).

- If the charges are dismissed or withdrawn or if you are let off with a reprimand, the record will be closed after two months.

- If you are found guilty but get a discharge, the record will be closed one year after you were found guilty if it is an absolute discharge and three years after if it's a conditional discharge.

- If you are convicted of a summary offence, the record will stay open for three years after you complete your sentence; if you are convicted of an indictable offence, it will stay open for five years.

- If you are 18 or older and commit another offence during the time in which your youth record is still open, that record will become part of your adult record and will never be closed unless a record suspension is granted.

- In addition to youth records, the RCMP keeps records of certain violent offences. In these records, an indictable offence may be listed for five years beyond the standard five-year period for indictable offences. In the case of a serious violent offence for which an adult sentence has been sought, that record can be kept open indefinitely (YCJA, s. 120[3]).

Once a youth record is closed, it will either be destroyed or archived for research purposes (in which case it will no longer identify you). For all intents and purposes, the law treats you as if you had never committed the crime. Your youth record will not appear on a criminal record check; its closure will happen automatically, and it will not be necessary to get a record suspension to seal it. In effect, you will be given the chance to start all over with a clean slate.

If you have an open record, one thing that you should be careful about is travelling to the United States. Both Canada and the United States have laws that give them the right to refuse entry to people from other countries who have a criminal record. The Canadian Police Information Centre (CPIC), which is operated by the RCMP, shares Canadian criminal record information with the National Crime Information Center in the United States, and US Customs and Border Protection has access to this information. If, when you try to cross the border, American border guards check the CPIC database and discover that you have an open criminal record, you can be arrested, detained at the border, and questioned. You will probably be sent back to Canada and told not to come to the United States again. Furthermore, if you are travelling by car (whether your own or someone else's), that car can be confiscated.

Although the RCMP does not share information on youth records that have been closed, if you travelled even once to the United States with an open record, border authorities may have accessed your record (whether or not you were refused entry) and still have it on file. Once they have that information, they can deny you entry into the United States on a later visit, even if that visit occurs after Canadian authorities have closed your record (or have issued a record suspension, if you were sentenced as an adult).[8] Unfortunately, because US authorities have access to the CPIC system, it is not entirely impossible that at some point they obtained records that contained information about your conviction (even if you didn't attempt to cross the border). All in all, then, your best defence against possible future trouble is simply never to travel to the United States with an open criminal record.

Civil Liability

Besides criminal law, another branch of law, known as *tort law*, also deals with offences. A **tort** is a wrongful act of some sort, generally one that involves personal injury or damage to someone's property. Although tort law derives largely (though not entirely) from the common law tradition, many torts are in fact crimes. Simply put, if the cause of the injury or damage was a criminal offence, such as assault or arson, then the tort is also a crime. The difference comes in the purpose of taking legal action. Under criminal law, lawsuits are brought by the Crown, not by the victim of the crime, and the goal is to punish the offender. Tort law differs in that the focus falls on the person who has been wronged,

---

8 In such a situation, your only option is to apply for a Waiver of Inadmissibility from US Customs and Border Protection, which, if granted, would allow you to enter the United States for a limited period of time. But the application fee is currently $585 in US dollars, and the process can take as long as a year. For further information, see "Applying for Waiver," *U.S. Customs and Border Protection,* https://help.cbp.gov/app/answers/detail/a_id/760/~/applying-for-waiver--person-entering-into-the-united-states-with-criminal.

on whose behalf the lawsuit is brought, and the goal is to gain some form of compensation, usually financial, for the injury or loss.

So if you injure someone or damage another person's property, you may or may not be charged with a crime, but the injured person may *sue* you—that is, take you to court and ask for damages (that is, compensation) for the wrong done. When the compensation awarded consists of a sum of money, the amount will depend on how much damage the court can be convinced was done. Ultimately, though, the amount of money that the injured person actually receives will depend on whether the guilty party is able to pay the full amount of the award. Since lawsuits are expensive, the standard wisdom is that it's not worth suing someone who really doesn't have much money.

When it comes to how much liability minors have for damages, the law is not very specific. According to common law, in order to be held responsible for damages, a child must have a certain minimum understanding of his or her actions, which children are presumed to lack prior to the age of about 6 or 7. As children grow older, courts are more likely to hold them responsible for their actions, but precisely how responsible depends on the situation. If you injure a person or someone's property while you are doing some "adult" activity, such as driving or snowmobiling, a court may well assume that you are relatively mature and should therefore bear greater responsibility for what happened. All the same, if a lawsuit against a young person is successful, the youth might not have the money to pay the damages—although if the young person is able to pay, he or she must do so.

 Are my parents responsible for damages I owe?

It depends. Under common law, parents are not automatically liable for damage their children have caused. They may be liable, however, if they didn't prevent you from causing damage when they could reasonably have done so, or if they gave you a dangerous object (such as a gun) that could clearly cause harm, or if the damage happened because you were performing a task that they told you to do.

In addition to common law provisions, some provinces have passed statutes, such as Ontario's Parental Responsibility Act, that give parents some liability for their children's actions. For example, according to section 2 of that act, if a child under 18 takes, damages, or destroys property worth no more than $25,000 (the maximum amount that can be claimed in Small Claims Court), the parents are liable to pay for the damage and for any economic loss resulting from the damage. However, if they can convince the court that they were exercising a reasonable degree of supervision over the child at the time (or that someone they had designated was) and had taken reasonable steps to prevent the child from engaging in the activity that caused the damage, then they cannot be held liable. Nor are they liable if the action that caused the damage or loss was not intentional.

In other words, the law recognizes that, even when parents have done their best to teach their children right from wrong, young people sometimes do damage that their parents could not have foreseen or prevented. Under those circumstances, it wouldn't really be fair to make parents pay for the damage, even if their own child was at fault.

As should go without saying, we hope you will never have need for the information we have presented in this chapter. Of course, everyone breaks the rules occasionally, but committing a crime is another matter. Even though the Youth Criminal Justice Act tries to be gentle with young offenders (at least up to a point), there is no doubt that getting in trouble with the law—being arrested, appearing in court, and possibly having to endure a punishment—is a potentially traumatic experience, one that could have long-lasting consequences. It is also important to remember that your rights end where other people's rights begin. When you knowingly commit a crime, you are basically saying that you don't care about other people's rights—which makes it hard to argue that you deserve to have your own rights respected. If, instead, you show that you understand why laws exist and are prepared to obey them, you will be in a stronger position to ask that youth be given more rights.

FIGHTING FOR YOUR RIGHTS

In this book, we have tried to give you a clear understanding of your rights under the law. If you started reading it looking for answers to specific questions, we hope you have found them. More generally, you will probably have realized that, although you are not without legal rights, those that allow you to make your own decisions or that require adults to respect your wishes are very limited, even if they do exist. Are you disappointed by this? We are. We wrote this book because we believe that children and teenagers are people like everyone else and that adults should not be able to make decisions for them based only on what adults want or simply as a way of asserting their power. Rather, in making decisions, parents should put their child's interests ahead of their own. We also believe that, as far as possible, youth should be able to make their own decisions, depending on how mature they are. The law should not consider them incapable of making choices independently simply because they are under some magic age. Similarly, we think that young people should be given more opportunities to do things normally done only by adults, if they can show they are able to do those things responsibly. In short, we are not happy with how the law sees young people.

At the moment, not everyone in Canada shares our views. Even people who talk a lot about human rights may not take a serious interest in children's and youth rights. Those who are concerned with children's rights tend to think more about protecting youth—often by limiting what they can or cannot do—than about giving them power over their own lives. On the whole, people still seem to think that young people really aren't able to make sensible decisions and that it should be up to adults to decide how much freedom they should have. But you don't have to automatically agree with them. You can form your own opinions about what rights the law should give to young people. And if you feel like it, you can even try to fight to change some of the laws that limit your rights.

It Doesn't Necessarily Have to Be This Way

Limits on the rights of youth are such a normal part of life that it may seem as if no one would ever see a reason to change them. But history suggests that this need not be so. Young people, in Canada as in many other places, used to have even fewer rights than they have today, as we have shown in previous chapters. Laws *are* changed from time to time, and this happens partly because people who care about something become convinced that existing laws are unfair. While, in many countries, the law cares much less about the rights of youth than it does in Canada, there are also a few places in the world that care more about their rights than our society does, and this can be seen in some of their laws. Take Norway, for instance. Here are some of the important rules in Norway's Children Act:

- According to section 30 of this law, the child "is entitled to care and consideration" from his or her parents and "must not be subjected to violence or in any other way be treated so as to harm or endanger his or her physical or mental health. This shall also apply when violence is carried out in connection with the child's upbringing. Use of violence and frightening or annoying behaviour or other inconsiderate conduct towards the child is prohibited." Among other things, this means that any form of corporal punishment is forbidden.

- Section 31 of the Children Act gives parents and others involved with the child the duty to listen to the child's opinions regarding decisions that affect him or her and to take those opinions into account, especially from the time the child reaches the age of 7. From the age of 12, the child's opinions should carry significant weight.

- Nor is parental authority absolute. According to section 33, parents "shall steadily extend the child's right to make his or her own decisions as he or she gets older and until he or she reaches the age of 18." Specifically, section 32 says that young people aged 15 and over "shall themselves decide the question of choice of education and of applying for membership of or resigning from associations." This provision recognizes that older children are ready to pursue their own interests and have their own ideas.

Norway's Children Act gives the country's young people significant rights that are also entirely within reason. Above all, it treats children and youth like independent individuals, as opposed to parents' possessions, and it views them as capable, rather than as incompetent. Why can't we incorporate similar rights into Canada's laws? We can if enough people are interested in doing so and can persuade enough politicians (the people who write bills and pass them into law) that children deserve more respect than they generally get.

Whatever rules you want changed, they will not change on their own: it will take work. If you want rights, you need to be ready to fight for them. So what are some of the things you can do?

FACT FILE   How Does Change Happen?

We tend to take the rights we have today for granted. Yet many of these rights are relatively recent: they weren't always there. Someone—usually those who had been denied these rights—had to fight for them. In 1976, one of us (Marvin) collaborated with June Callwood, a celebrated social rights activist, to write a book called *The Law Is Not for Women,* a guide similar to this one. It told women what rights the law gave them, but it also explained what rights they didn't have. This book was written at a time when the law in Canada still did not treat the sexes equally. Even in 1976, in most provinces a husband still had the right to decide where the whole family should live. If the wife refused to live where he chose, he could go to court and accuse her of deserting him, and she could lose the rights she had as his wife! This was only one of many sexist laws that still existed at that time, although such laws were already being challenged. Today, men and women are seen as equal under the law. This change did not happen overnight, however. Women—along with men who agreed with their views—had to work hard to convince people that women should not be regarded as inferior to men and that laws should be changed to reflect this equality. In the same way, the idea that youth should be given more rights than they currently have is still new and strange for many people. If young people got together and put a similar effort into working to gain additional legal rights, they might gradually persuade more and more adults to back the idea. And, with the support of these adults, they might end up convincing lawmakers to give them those rights.

Get Organized

To be honest, you are unlikely to change anything on your own. A lone voice is usually not enough to convince law-makers that something needs to change. What's required is interest and encouragement from the public. When a lot of people stand up and make their voices heard together, politicians will usually listen. So if you want lawmakers to take a serious interest in giving youth more legal rights, you need to connect with other young people who want to work for the same cause and, if possible, find some adults who want to help. To learn how to form an organization to promote your goals, you can begin by finding out about other activists and special interest groups and look at what they do and how they talk, write, and behave. In other words, you don't have to start from scratch.

Talk to Others

Before going public with your ideas, think of what you can do to influence the people right around you. First of all, try talking about your legal rights with your brothers and sisters, friends, schoolmates, and other people you know who are about your age. You can share what you have learned from this book and make them aware of what rights the law gives youth and what rights it denies them. This sharing of information can lead to an exchange of opinions and ideas with other young people about what rights you *should* have. Finally, you can encourage them to join you in working for children's and youth rights.

Eventually, you may want to start sharing your ideas with adults. Even if you do not feel comfortable doing so right away, sooner or later, your parents and other adults close to you will likely figure out that you're interested in youth rights. Their initial reaction to your opinions and activities may be good or bad, but you will be more likely to be taken seriously if you stick to the following principles:

- You show that you appreciate the adults in your life and that your opinions are not meant to insult them.

- You show that you have thought about your ideas and are committed to them.

- You are prepared with strong arguments.

- You speak calmly and respectfully.

- You are willing to listen to opposite arguments and be polite when arguing against them.

At some point, you may wish to try to convince your parents that you are entitled to more rights and that they should give you more freedom. In this case, you'll need to step carefully. It is difficult to change the opinions of adults about their way of raising their children and easy to make them angry by challenging their authority as parents. Therefore, not only should you be well prepared, but you should also start any conversations about this topic positively, politely, and diplomatically. Try to choose a moment for starting the discussion when both you and your parents are calm and in a good mood, and do so in such a way that it doesn't seem like you're looking for an argument. You could, for instance, say that you appreciate your parents' efforts in raising you but are not happy with some of their restrictions, and while you realize they have your own good in mind, you would like them to listen to your opinions as to why you deserve to be more in control of your own choices.

If you do decide to begin such a conversation, you will want to be ready with strong arguments and be able to present them well to your parents. We'd also suggest that, before you try raising this subject at home, you ask some of your friends whether they've had such discussions with their parents and, if so, what they said that their parents found convincing. We hope that your arguments will be successful, but be prepared for your parents not to have much sympathy for your desire for more rights. Although adults were all children themselves once, many of them lose touch with their childhood and the feelings they had at the time. Even if they remember how they felt when they were young, they often see things from an adults-are-right point of view, and many of them also feel entitled to the authority they have. If you speak politely, seriously, and without raising your voice, you will increase the chances that your parents will listen to you, and if you have good, mature arguments, they just might be willing to consider your opinions. Perhaps you may even have some suggestions about how this change could benefit your parents as well as yourself.

Unfortunately, not all parents are willing to listen to arguments from their children that challenge their own views. You will know whether your parents are generally willing to talk with you about your opinions or whether they're likely to resist your efforts to have a discussion. If you do talk to them about your rights and freedoms and they get angry at you for disagreeing with their rules or opinions, try to stay calm. As long as you are calm and polite, you have good grounds for asking your parents simply to allow you to express your opinion and to listen to what you're saying. It might also help to gently remind your parents that they probably had arguments with their own parents and probably felt unhappy if they weren't even allowed to say what they thought.

Meanwhile, remember that actions speak louder than words. Your parents—and other adults—may take your ideas more seriously if you show that, besides asking for rights, you are willing to be a good citizen and accept responsibility. In a conversation about making your own decisions, it might be very helpful if you are able to truthfully point out all the ways in which you already act responsibly. Perhaps you could remind them that you attend school regularly, or that you do your homework and try to get good grades in school; perhaps you have chores at home that you carry out in a responsible and trustworthy manner; perhaps you are reliably respectful and considerate of others. If you can show evidence of your maturity, this may help your parents take you seriously when you explain that you are not happy that, on one hand, you are expected to fulfill certain responsibilities, while, on the other hand, no one seems to be interested in letting you take more responsibility for your own choices.

Hopefully, you will be able to convince your parents or other adults you talk with to see things at least partly your way. Yet, despite your best efforts, you may not succeed, and in some cases you may not even manage to get them to listen to you. If this happens, you'd do well to back off and try to avoid further conflict—but don't let their anger and disapproval discourage you from having your own opinions or from being a youth rights activist.

Write

It's a good idea to get into the habit of writing about your ideas and the reasons behind them. If you are able to write convincing articles and essays, you can spread your ideas in many ways. For example, you can publish what you write in school newspapers, on websites, or as letters to the editor of a newspaper. Eventually, your writing might be read by important people who have influence in government, organizations, or the community and who can change things. Perhaps one day you will even publish a book.

Just like speaking about your ideas, writing effectively about your ideas requires that you have strong arguments to back them up. We suggest you try to get ideas both for what you will write about and how you will write it by reading what other people have written in support of children's and youth rights or in support of other civil rights, such as racial equality or women's rights. In order to sharpen your writing and persuasive skills, read good essays and use the opportunities you have at school to learn to write effective arguments.[1]

---

1 Two well-known essays you might start with are "The Subjection of Women," by John Stuart Mill (1869) and "Politics and the English

As you read examples of persuasive writing, you will learn ways of writing that can make a good impression on your reader. One thing to keep in mind about effective writing is the importance of adapting your writing style to your audience. If you write for other young people, you might choose to write in a lively, conversational style, whereas if you write to a politician, your style might be relatively serious and formal. When you write someone a formal letter or similar text, you should make sure you write politely and without showing angry emotions too strongly. For example, suppose it really bothers you that some schools make students wear uniforms, instead of letting them choose their own clothing. Here's an example of the sort of letter you might write to your provincial government:

> The Honourable Lisa M. Thompson, Minister of
> Education
> Mowat Block, 22nd Floor
> 900 Bay Street
> Toronto, ON M7A 1L2
> February 4, 2019
>
> Dear Minister,
>
> I am writing to you with a request to consider
> introducing an amendment to the Education Act,
> section 302(5) of which allows boards of education

Language," by George Orwell (1945). You can also look at the editorials in your local newspaper and try to figure out what makes some of them persuasive and others less so.

to make policies regarding "appropriate dress" in schools. As it stands, this section enables schools to require students to wear uniforms. In my opinion, school uniforms are an unwarranted infringement on students' liberty, and the arguments in favour of them are misguided. I would therefore ask you to take the initiative to have section 302(5) repealed.

Whatever reasons may be given for introducing school uniforms, there is no denying that they infringe on students' personal freedom and that they will therefore make many of them unhappy and resentful. Young people want to have choices like everybody else, especially on such personal matters as how they dress. If their freedom to choose their own clothing is to be restricted, there should be substantial reasons for doing so.

Some of those who favour school uniforms argue that they help to promote order and discipline. In the United States, especially, school uniforms have become an increasingly popular approach to issues surrounding violence and other disruptive behaviour. And yet, despite a number of research studies, no conclusive evidence exists to support the contention that uniforms actually do improve school discipline. Disciplinary problems occur in all schools, regardless of what students wear. Many factors contribute to such problems, and the idea that the solution lies simply in a change of clothing seems at best naïve. Proponents of school uniforms also claim that a strict dress code prevents young people from wearing clothing that is in some way provocative, which distracts them from their studies. At least in my experience, though, if students pay attention to each other's clothes, it is during breaks, not in class—and, in any case, life is full of potential distractions. Moreover, one suspects that it is teachers, not students, who find such attire distracting. Young people are in the process of defining who they are, and clothing is one of many ways in which people express their self-identity. I see no reason to deny students this opportunity.

Another popular argument in favour of school uniforms is that they put both wealthy and poor students on an equal level and head off the possibility that relatively affluent students will tease classmates whose parents cannot afford to buy them expensive or trendy clothes. Such teasing may indeed happen at times, but this seems an inadequate reason to limit students' freedom of dress. When I was a student, I would far rather have dealt with my peers' criticism of my clothing than have adults "solve" the problem by telling me and everyone else how to dress. In fact, I would argue that this solution is actually counterproductive, in that it attempts to shield students from unpleasant experiences. Learning how to deal constructively with social differences prepares young people for the adult world, where inequalities between people do exist and are not artificially suppressed.

School uniforms can be counterproductive in another way as well. By insisting on regulating their appearance, authorities are giving young people yet another reason to dislike school. Strict rules increase the likelihood that students will learn to resent adult authority and may well result in rebellion against the offending rule—thereby obliging teachers to waste time enforcing it. In other words, demanding that students wear uniforms merely creates a new issue with regard to discipline.

In short, it is difficult to find a reasonable justification for school uniforms. Indeed, I would argue that the wearing of uniforms satisfies adult needs more than it benefits students. School uniforms have traditionally been associated with upscale private schools: they were markers of privilege. Today, they seem to have become a form of branding—a way for schools to set themselves apart from other schools as something "special," as if parents now feel that sending their child to an ordinary public school just isn't good enough. This is the opposite of the spirit of equality on which public education was founded. I therefore ask that you consider making efforts to repeal section 302(5) of the Education Act. By doing so, your government will demonstrate its commitment not only to equity but to the rights of young people to be independent human beings.

I hope you will take my views into consideration.

Sincerely,

Ned Lecic

Use the Internet

If you wish to advocate for youth rights, consider creating a website. In fact, if you form a children's and youth rights organization, a website is a must. But you could also create your own blog, complete with FAQ pages and external links. Then you'll need to use social media to direct traffic to your website. Get active on Twitter and create a Facebook page, with a link to your website, and update it regularly with brief but interesting posts. You can also make creative use of Instagram.

Your website should be well designed and the material on it accurate and well written. If you don't have a lot of visual talent, perhaps you know someone who does. Above all, have a good, critical look at other websites that promote human and civil rights.[2] What do you like about them, and

---

2 Two of our favourites are the websites of the National Youth Rights Association, which is based in the US (https://www.youthrights.org/), and of the Global Initiative to End All Corporal Punishment of Children (https://endcorporalpunishment.org/), an organization based in the UK. Visually, they're quite different, but both are well laid out, informative, and persuasive.

what don't you like? Is the information they provide clear and useful? What makes you want to stay on a site, and what do you find irritating? When it comes to websites, examples are probably the best teachers.

Talk to Lawmakers and Get Involved in the Community

One way to change laws is to deal directly with those who make them. Anyone can telephone or write a letter or an e-mail to a member of Parliament, a member of the provincial legislature, or a town or band councillor. You can also arrange to meet with one of these lawmakers so that you can share your thoughts about how the law treats youth and ask for his or her support in getting a law changed. In this case, before you set up an appointment, think about which level of government makes laws about the issue you wish to discuss. MPs deal with federal laws (such as the Youth Criminal Justice Act or the Cannabis Act), MLAs make laws about provincial or territorial matters such as education and family law, and city or band councillors deal with local policies such as curfews. Although it's usual to talk to the MP or MLA in your own electoral district, if you've heard or read about a politician who seems interested in the rights and interests of young people or has a history of supporting causes similar to your own, then get in touch with that person.

Political officials tend to be busy people, so you need to be respectful of their time. If you meet with one of them, you should be clear about what you are asking them to do and be well prepared with good arguments to back up your request. It would also be helpful to have some sort of evidence (such as a letter of support from an adult—that is, someone old enough to vote) that other people agree with your position. Bear in mind as well that lawmakers tend to be conservative: rarely are they willing to consider extreme changes. So you will have a better chance of success—at least in the long run—if you are realistic in what you ask for. For example, you might just be able to convince an MP to support the idea that 16-year-olds should be allowed to vote, but no politician today is likely to favour abolishing the voting age altogether.

It would be nice if the person with whom you've met immediately showed an interest in changing the law. But don't be surprised when this doesn't happen. A lot of lobbying will no doubt be required to change social attitudes and convince politicians that youth deserve to have more rights and to be allowed more responsibility than the law presently gives them. But even if, on your first try, a lawmaker seems to dismiss your ideas, at least he or she will have learned that you're not happy with the rights you currently have. If more and more young people complain about their lack of rights, eventually lawmakers will begin to listen. After all, if nothing else, today's young people are tomorrow's voters.

Finally, it's always a good idea to find out about what is going on in your city or community and what issues are important at the moment. Sometimes, when a government is considering a new law or an amendment to an existing one, it holds a public consultation so that people can voice their opinions on the proposed legislation before it is passed. Even if the law in question doesn't particularly relate to issues that you are concerned about, participating in public consultations is a great way to get a sense of how government works, and it also gives you experience in expressing your views. Becoming an active member of a local association may likewise help you to gain recognition in your community. If you live in a big city, you might want to start by focusing on your local electoral district or even just on the neighbourhood where you live. That makes it a lot easier to build relationships and exert some influence on those in power.

Write Petitions

The greater the number of people who support a change in the law, the more likely it is that lawmakers will pay attention. There's nothing wrong with talking to politicians or writing letters to them yourself, but drawing up a petition and getting people to sign it is a powerful way to show that an idea has broad public support. In a petition, you write an opening statement that clearly describes what law you want changed, followed by a brief, well-written explanation of why this change needs to be made and what it would accomplish. You then "circulate" the petition: you show it to as many people as possible and ask whether they'd be willing to sign it. Be prepared to explain more about the issue underlying the petition and to answer questions that people may have. If they agree to sign the petition, they simply write their name and address and then their signature on a line under the letter.

Once you've collected as many names as you think you can get, you send the petition to a senior member of government. Depending on the law in question, this could be the prime minister, the premier of the province or territory in which you live, or your city or town mayor. But it's often even better to send the petition directly to the government minister whose department is responsible for administering the law that you're trying to have changed. For example, if you live in British Columbia and are hoping to change a rule in the BC School Act, send your petition to the BC Minister of Education. If you live in Québec and are seeking an amendment to one of the articles in the Civil Code about parental authority, send your petition to Québec's Minister of Families. If you're trying to get the Canada Elections Act changed to lower the voting age, send your petition to the federal Minister of Justice. You can also use petitions as a means to persuade any other government agency, organization, or institution (such as your school) to change its current policies.

You can talk to people around you about signing your petition, but you may also want to send copies of it to people you know who live elsewhere and who support your efforts. That way, they can work on convincing even more people to sign it—although, if your petition concerns a provincial or territorial law, it's best if the people who sign it live in that province or territory (or, if it's a municipal law, in that municipality). It's also worth trying to get some media attention for your petition, partly so that people who might be interested in signing it will know that it exists. In addition, some positive publicity will make it harder for politicians or other people in power to ignore the issue that the petition concerns.

Petitions can also be organized online, on Facebook or change.org (among other websites). The obvious advantage to an online petition is numbers: it lets you reach out to a great many people. At least initially, the disadvantage was some people didn't think that online petitions were as trustworthy as actual pieces of paper—although online petitions have become very common today. If you do start a petition on the Internet, however, be sure to ask the people who sign it to provide their full names and addresses, so that your petition won't raise doubts about whether some of the signatures were made up. To send the petition to the lawmaker or other official who needs to see it, you can either write the person a formal e-mail, with a link to the petition in it, or mail a printout of the petition and its signatures to his or her office, along with a letter containing the link.

Invoke the UN Convention on the Rights of the Child

Even though the UN Convention on the Rights of the Child doesn't have the status of law in Canada, we are supposed to abide by its principles, and it offers a potentially powerful means of persuasion. It makes sense, then, to get to know what rights the Convention gives to young people. If you are writing to someone, you can quote one or more of its articles and explain how the change that you are requesting will support your rights under those articles. Invoking the Convention is another way of adding more voices to your own—in this case, the voice of the United Nations. If your activities ever get as far as lobbying for major legal change at the federal level, you might petition lawmakers to incorporate some of the rights spelled out in the Convention into existing Canadian laws, so that these rights will be legally enforceable.

Challenge a Law in Court

If you think that an existing law contains a rule about young people that violates your constitutional rights, you can—in theory—file a lawsuit in hopes of having that portion of the law overturned. We are including this possibility because it does exist, but we have to admit that it would be an extremely difficult undertaking. For one thing, before you did anything else, you would want to talk to a lawyer about the chances that such a lawsuit would succeed—that is, about whether a legal case could actually be made. (A lawyer might know, for example, that the rule in question has already been challenged in court and was judged to be constitutional.) Moreover, even if, in a lawyer's opinion, the constitutionality of the rule could reasonably be questioned, bringing such a challenge yourself would be extraordinarily expensive, especially if the case went to the

Supreme Court. You would need to hire a very experienced lawyer, and, assuming that you are still a minor, you would also need to find a litigation guardian to file the lawsuit for you (as we explained in chapter 2).

A more realistic option is to try to enlist the support of an organization that deals with children's and youth rights or related issues and has a history of activism. Such an organization is likely to have access to legal counsel, with whom it could consult. If the organization became convinced that the rule in question could indeed be unconstitutional, it might be willing to bring a lawsuit itself and/or on your behalf.

Demonstrate

Section 2 of the Charter of Rights and Freedoms gives citizens the right to "freedom of peaceful assembly" and "freedom of association." Among other things, this means that people are allowed to get together in a public place and protest against something, as long as they don't damage property or do anything that is dangerous, violent, or otherwise illegal. Holding a demonstration—waving placards and shouting slogans—has long been a popular way to focus attention on a cause. It can be an effective tactic provided you can get enough people to take part in it, so if you're planning a demonstration, it needs to be well advertised beforehand. Other than just telling your friends about it, you can hand out flyers or put up posters in places where those who might want to participate tend to be found. And, of course, you can spread the word on social media. A day or two before the demonstration, you might also want to let the local media (especially newspapers) know when and where it will be happening.

Where you hold your demonstration will depend on what you are demonstrating about. If you are protesting against a provincial law, you can demonstrate in front of the provincial legislature (if you happen to live in the capital city) or else some other government building, such as a court of justice. If you're protesting against a local bylaw, demonstrate in front of city hall. If you object to a company business policy, you can protest in front of their headquarters or other property (such as a store), as long as you don't trespass on private property. You could even hold a noontime demonstration in front of your school or board of education building, if you're protesting against a school policy.

Demonstrations often begin with a march through the streets, from a chosen gathering place to a final destination. But, regardless of whether they include a march, demonstrations need to be carefully planned. They also need to be led by someone (or by a small group of leaders), partly to make sure that they don't get out of hand. If protestors start physically assaulting people or damaging property, what began as a peaceful demonstration could turn into a riot, which is dangerous (and also illegal). If a protest seems to be getting unruly, the police are likely to show up and order everyone to "disperse" in order to break up the demonstration, and they may even arrest people. If ever you are involved in a demonstration where this happens, obey police orders immediately. You can get into serious trouble if you don't.

Get Help When You Need It

Standing up for your rights takes courage, and it can sometimes be risky. This is especially true when you are dealing with institutional authorities, such as the people who run a school or a hospital or a foster care facility, and asking them to respect the rights you are supposed to have. In some cases, the only people to whom you can direct a complaint are the same people who are violating your rights, and they may try to punish you for complaining about their behaviour. Moreover, individual institutions (such as a public school) are often part of much larger systems, including ones run by the government. Those in charge of such institutions will know how this system is set up and may be able to use it to their advantage. If you accuse them of not respecting your rights, they may, for instance, refer the matter to someone higher up, who will probably support them rather than you.

Such negative reactions should not discourage you from fighting for your rights, but, before you begin, it is wise to think about what you're up against and what might happen. In an uneven fight, it helps to have someone who will back you up. This could be a parent, but it could also be another adult whom you trust, preferably one who holds a professional position of some sort, as such people tend to have more influence. Also, if the institution in question is part of the government, you could take your complaint to a child ombudsman or youth advocate, who might in turn arrange for a lawyer to help you. If you ever find yourself dealing with the staff of an institution who seem unwilling to respect your rights, be sure to keep a written record of what you're experiencing, including any documents issued to you. That way, if you decide to take action, you can use these records as evidence of how you were (or are) treated.

Don't Lose Touch with Your Youthful Spirit

Since the idea of youth rights is still fairly new, changing anything is likely to take a long time and require a lot of effort. But don't be discouraged: nothing will change if you don't try to make your voice heard. As long as there is someone out there who wants to change something and is willing to work toward it, hope is alive. If a lot of young people get together, find at least a few adults who are on their side, and keep arguing that youth deserve more rights, eventually the broader public will begin to pay attention, and attitudes will shift, as they have many times in the past.

To all of you who decide to join the cause of children's and youth rights, we wish you success in your efforts. We believe that the movement for youth rights will continue to grow, but by the time big changes start to happen, you may already be grown up, and the restrictions you've been fighting against won't apply to you any more. We hope that you will hang onto your commitment to youth rights even after you are no longer a youth yourself. Just because you're now an independent adult doesn't mean you have to lose touch with what it felt like to be a young person—with the sense of possibility but also with the struggles and frustrations. In the future, you may be a parent yourself, or a teacher, or perhaps even a lawmaker, and you will be able to affect the lives of the next generation of youth. We hope that you use the rights that you gain as an adult to increase their rights, as youth.

GLOSSARY OF LEGAL TERMS

Access: The extent to which a court allows a parent who does not have custody of a child to see the child and be given important information about him or her.

Acquit: To find someone not guilty of a crime in court.

Age of majority: The age at which the law treats you as an adult (in Canada, 18 or 19, depending on the jurisdiction).

Appeal: To challenge the decision of a court in a higher court.

Bill: A proposal for a new law or for an amendment to an old law, before the Parliament or legislature passes it.

Binding: Unbreakable or non-negotiable.

Case law: The law that is established by judges' opinions in court cases. See also *common law*.

Common law: A legal system inherited from England that allows judges to make rules of law through their decisions in court cases instead of having to rely on the statutes alone. See also *case law*.

Constitution: A law or set of laws in a state that provide the fundamental rules for how the state should function.

Convict: To find someone guilty of a crime in court.

Crown Attorney: A lawyer working for the government who prosecutes a person accused of a crime and tries to prove at his or her trial that he or she is guilty.

Custody: (1) The rights and duties that parents have to care for and make decisions about their minor children (sometimes called "guardianship"); (2) State control, that is, being locked up in jail or, in the case of a minor, being handed over to the care of the state.

Defendant: A person who is accused of a crime in criminal court or is being sued in civil court.

Discharge: When a person is found guilty of a lesser crime, the judge may decide to give him or her a discharge, which means he or she will not be convicted and sentenced.

Emancipation: In Québec law, when a court gives a minor many of the legal rights of an adult. Until then, the law considers a minor to be "unemancipated."

Federation (adj. **federal**): A country like Canada that is made up of provinces or states that have a constitutional right to make their own laws on certain subjects.

Indictable offence: A relatively serious criminal offence, usually carrying quite a heavy penalty.

International treaty: An agreement between two or more countries.

Jurisdiction: 1) A place such as a city, province, territory, or country that has the power to make laws about something. 2) The power a court has over someone or something.

Last will and testament: A document in which a person states what he or she wants to be done with his or her property when he or she dies. A parent may also name a guardian for his or her minor children in a will.

Legal capacity: The power to do legal acts such as sign a contract, buy things, or sue someone without the help or permission of a guardian. Until you reach the age of majority, you have some legal capacity, but not a great deal.

Litigation guardian: An adult who acts on behalf of a minor in court actions; can also be called a "guardian *ad litem*" or a "next friend."

Minor: Someone under the age of majority. Some laws use "child" or "infant" to mean the same thing.

Parole: When a person is released from his or her sentence early on condition of good behaviour.

Plaintiff: A person who sues someone in a civil court.

Plea (vb. to **plead/enter a plea**): If a person charged with a crime admits his or her guilt, the person pleads guilty. If the person claims to be innocent, he or she pleads not guilty.

Precedent: A rule laid out in a court decision, which is binding on that court and on lower courts until either that court or a higher court changes it.

Probation: When a person convicted of a crime is sentenced to a period under court surveillance but is not fined or sent to jail as long as the person keeps the conditions of the probation order.

Ratify: Officially agree to respect a convention, treaty, declaration, or charter. A country (sometimes referred to as a "State Party") ratifies an international treaty when its government declares that it will respect the treaty.

Regulation: An order given by the government or a minister giving rules that provide more details to those already given by a statute law.

Repudiate: To refuse to fulfill your side of a contract when the law allows you to do so.

Status offence: Something that is against the law only for a certain group of people who share the same status (such as something that is illegal for a youth to do but not for an adult).

Statute: Any written law passed by a parliament or legislature.

Subpoena (pronounced "suh-*pee*-na"): A paper ordering someone to come to court.

Summary offence: A relatively minor criminal offence, usually carrying a light penalty.

Tort: An offence involving personal injury or damage to someone's property.

Unconstitutional: The term used to describe a rule of law that goes against a rule in the Constitution and so is invalid.

Verdict: The decision of a court as to whether an accused person is guilty or not guilty.

Void: A court voids a contract when it declares it invalid.

Warrant: An order issued by a judge allowing the police (or another government official) to arrest someone, to take them into custody, or to search them or their property.

HOW A BILL BECOMES LAW

Our system of government is set out in the **Constitution** (https://laws-lois.justice.gc.ca/eng/const/), which has two main parts: the Constitution Act, 1867—formerly called the British North America Act, 1867—and the Constitution Act, 1982. The 1867 act founded the country now known as Canada by joining several British colonies into one federation. It describes the structure of Canada's government, and it also specifies what powers the federal government has and what powers the provinces have. Originally, the 1867 Constitution Act could be altered only by an act of the British Parliament, which meant that Britain had the final authority over the government of Canada. This changed in 1982, when Britain relinquished this authority and Canada "patriated" its constitution—that is, made it our own—so that our Parliament in Ottawa no longer had to seek approval from Britain in order to amend our constitution.

At that time, Canada passed a second act—the Constitution Act, 1982. It opens with an important list of rights for all Canadians, called the Charter of Rights and Freedoms, and it recognizes the special rights of the Indigenous peoples who live in the country that settlers named Canada.[1] The 1982 act

---

1 The 1982 Constitution Act uses the term "aboriginal" peoples, who are defined as First Nations, Inuit, and Métis individuals, but "Indigenous" is the preferred term today.

also lays out a procedure for amending the Constitution and lists all the legal acts, orders, and amendments from 1867 to 1982 that the Constitution incorporates. All other laws made in Canada must follow the rules set out in the Constitution, or else they are **unconstitutional** and therefore invalid. For that reason, by including the Charter of Rights and Freedoms, our Constitution ensures that no future government of Canada can pass a law that violates our basic human and political rights.

The part of the 1982 Constitution Act that recognizes Indigenous rights is often called "section 35" (although it also includes a section 35.1). In addition, section 25 states that the Charter of Rights and Freedoms cannot be interpreted in a way that would limit Indigenous rights. Section 35 defines Indigenous peoples as First Nations, Inuit, and Métis. At the same time, the Constitution does not attempt to define what qualifies as an Indigenous right, as doing so would be too "prescriptive"—that is, it would impose a particular interpretation. Instead, the Constitution leaves it to the courts to decide, with regard to specific cases, whether something is or is not an Indigenous right.

The laws passed by Parliament or by provincial or territorial legislatures are called statutes. Any new statute starts its life as a bill—a proposal for either a new law or an amendment (change) to an existing one. At the federal level, most bills begin in the House of Commons, and most of these are government bills, introduced by government ministers, although any member of Parliament (MP) can introduce a bill, in which case it is called a private member's bill. A bill may, however, start out in the Senate, rather than the House; this will usually be a private member's bill, introduced by an individual senator, although sometimes it's a government bill. A government bill typically reflects the platform on which that government was elected—the policies and the program of action that it put before voters. For the most part, private members' bills also relate to matters of public policy, but they may also reflect the special concerns and interests of a particular group of people.

When a bill is introduced into the House, it must go through a number of steps in order to become law. First, it receives a first reading, just to introduce it. Next, it is given a second reading, during which it is discussed and debated. The House may vote to reject it at this point, although this seldom happens with government bills. After its second reading, the bill is usually referred to one of the House's standing committees—whichever one specializes in the topic most closely related to the bill. (For example, a bill about refugee policy would probably go to the Standing Committee on Citizenship and Immigration.)[2] The members of this committee study the bill and may make recommendations for amending it or even rejecting it. If the committee recommends any amendments, the entire House will consider these during the report stage, when MPs examine the report submitted by the committee. At this stage, other MPs may also suggest their own amendments. Next, the bill gets a third reading, in which the House votes to adopt the bill in its original form, to adopt it with one or more of the suggested amendments, or to completely reject it.

Once a bill is adopted by the House, it passes to the Senate, which will decide to adopt or reject it using the same steps as in the House: first reading, second reading, committee and report stages, and third reading. If the bill is passed by the Senate, it is sent to the Governor General for Royal Assent. He

2 A *standing* committee is one that has already been struck—that is, set up—and that meets regularly to study a particular area of government policy. A list of House committees is available at https://www.ourcommons.ca/ Committees/en/List. Although a bill is usually referred to a standing committee, it may instead be sent to a legislative committee, one that has been created on a short-term basis to consider the bill. (Committees that are struck temporarily for a specific purpose are called *ad hoc* committees.)

or she has the power either to approve the bill ("give assent"), at which point it becomes law, to withhold assent, at which point the bill fails, or to ask the Queen to make the final decision. But no Governor General of Canada has ever refused to assent to a bill passed by Parliament, and it is unlikely that one would do so without an extremely good reason (for example, if he or she thought a bill was unconstitutional). After Royal Assent is given, a government newspaper called the *Canada Gazette* (now available only in electronic form) publishes the law, making it official.[3]

Senators' bills follow all the same steps, except that they are first debated in the Senate and are then sent to the House. In either case, both the Senate and the House must pass the bill or it will not become law. Usually, senators do not reject bills that have already been passed by the House, although occasionally they do use this power.

Provincial and territorial bills follow a similar process except that the legislature has only one house: there is no senate. A bill that passes three readings in the legislature is sent for Royal Assent to the Lieutenant Governor (or, in the territories, to the commissioner), who may give assent, refuse to give it, or (except in the case of territorial commissioners) ask the Governor General to decide on the bill. Although Canada's history is full of occasions on which a province's Lieutenant Governor rejected a bill or referred it to the Governor General for a decision, this has not happened since 1961.

---

3 The version in the *Gazette* is the official one, meaning that if someone else publishes a version with a mistake in it, you have to follow the law as written in the *Gazette*. The full versions of federal laws on the Department of Justice website are also official. However, versions in professional sources such as CanLII (http://www.canlii.org/), while not official, should normally also be correct.

Turning a bill into a law is a long, complicated, and some-times frustrating process. But changing the law is a serious matter, and the right thing to do isn't always obvious. So it's good that a lot of thought and discussion goes into creating or amending a law.

USEFUL RESOURCES

Children's Rights Websites

- Canadian Children's Rights Council
- The Convention on the Rights of the Child

Legal Information and Help

- Canadian Legal Information Institute: contains most of Canada's laws and many court judgments.

- The Charter of Rights and Freedoms

- Children's Legal and Educational Resource Centre: a youth legal rights information website run by a Calgary-based youth legal clinic.

- Department of Justice of Canada: contains useful information on family law, criminal justice, and Canada's system of justice.

- Éducaloi: detailed website about Québec law; includes youth pages.

- Families Change: useful advice for youth whose parents are divorcing; run by the Justice Education Society of BC but with information on every province and territory.

- Justice for Children and Youth: JFCY is a free, non-profit legal aid clinic in Ontario; for young people under 18 and homeless youth under 25; site includes information about legal rights and blog.

- Legal Aid of Montreal | Laval: website published by *Centre communautaire juridique de Montréal*, a law firm that helps youth; website contains articles on legal issues.

- Ontario Office of the Children's Lawyer

- Society for Children and Youth of BC: non-profit Vancouver children's and youth rights organization; includes legal assistance (Child and Youth Legal Centre).

Child Protection Agencies (Social Services)

Please note: each province or territory organizes its social services in different ways. This list of departments and agencies should not be taken as comprehensive.

Indigenous Services Canada

- First Nations Child and Family Services

Social Services by Province and Territory

- Alberta Ministry of Children's Services
- British Columbia Child Protection Services
- Manitoba Child and Family Services
- New Brunswick Child Protection Services

- Newfoundland and Labrador Department of Children, Seniors and Social Development
- Northwest Territories Child Protection Services (Yellowknife Health and Social Services Authority)
- Nova Scotia Department of Community Services
- Nunavut Children and Family Services
- Ontario Association of Children's Aid Societies (Locate a Children's Aid Society)
- Prince Edward Island Child Protection Services
- Québec Director of Youth Protection
- Saskatchewan Child Protection
- Yukon Family and Children's Services

Children's Advocates and Ombudsmen

- Alberta Office of the Child and Youth Advocate
- British Columbia Representative for Children and Youth
- Manitoba Office of the Children's Advocate
- New Brunswick Office of the Child and Youth Advocate
- Newfoundland Advocate for Children and Youth
- Nova Scotia Youth Ombudsman
- Nunavut Representative for Children and Youth
- Ontario Ombudsman (as of May 2019, there is no longer a provincial advocate for children and youth)
- Québec—*Commission des droits de la personne et des droits de la jeunesse*
- Saskatchewan Advocate for Children and Youth
- Yukon Child Advocate Office

LEGISLATION, CONVENTIONS, CHARTERS, AND COURT CASES

International Conventions, Declarations, and Legislation

- Children Act (Norway)
- Convention on the Rights of the Child
- United Nations Declaration on the Rights of Indigenous Peoples
- Universal Declaration of Human Rights

National Legislation

- Canada Business Corporations Act
- Canada Labour Code
- Canadian Human Rights Act
- Cannabis Act
- Charter of Rights and Freedoms
- Civil Marriage Act
- Constitution
- Controlled Drugs and Substances Act
- Criminal Code

- Firearms Act
- Indian Act
- National Defence Act
- Youth Criminal Justice Act

Provincial Legislation

Alberta

- Child, Youth and Family Enhancement Act
- Employment Standards Code
- Employment Standards Regulation
- Family Law Act

British Columbia

- Child, Family and Community Service Act
- Employment Standards Act
- Employment Standards Regulation
- Family Law Act
- Infants Act

Manitoba

- Child and Family Services Act
- Employment Standards Code
- Family Maintenance Act

New Brunswick

- Employment Standards Act
- Family Services Act

- **Newfoundland and Labrador**
- Children's Law Act
- Family Law Act
- Labour Standards Act
- Wills Act

Northwest Territories

- Children's Law Act
- Employment Standards Act

Nova Scotia

- Children and Family Services Act
- Labour Standards Code
- Parenting and Support Act (formerly the Maintenance and Custody Act)

Nunavut

- Children's Law Act
- Employment of Young Persons Regulations

Ontario

- Age of Majority and Accountability Act
- Child, Youth, and Family Services Act, 2017
- Children's Law Reform Act
- College of Teachers Act, 1996
- Education Act
- Family Law Act
- Human Rights Code

- Marriage Act
- Occupational Health and Safety Act
- Parental Responsibility Act, 2000
- Provincial Offences Act
- Regulation 194: Rules of Civil Procedure
- Regulation 258/98: Rules of the Small Claims Court

Prince Edward Island

- Family Law Act
- Youth Employment Act

Québec

- Act Respecting Labour Standards
- Civil Code
- Education Act

Saskatchewan

- Child and Family Services Act
- Conditions of Employment Regulations
- Family Maintenance Act, 1997

Yukon

- Child and Family Services Act
- Employment Standards Act

Appendix D

Court Cases

A.B. v. C.D. and E. F., 2019 BSCS 254

A.C. v. Manitoba (Director of Child and Family Services), 2009 SCC 30 (CanLII)—HTTPS://WWW.CANLII.ORG/EN/CA/SCC/DOC/2009/2009SCC30/2009SCC30.HTML

Antrobus v. Antrobus, 2009 BCSC 1341 (CanLII)—HTTPS://WWW.CANLII.ORG/EN/BC/BCSC/DOC/2009/2009BCSC1341/2009BCSC1341.HTML

B. (R.) v. Children's Aid Society of Metropolitan Toronto, 1995 CanLII 115 (SCC)—HTTPS://WWW.CANLII.ORG/EN/CA/SCC/DOC/1995/1995CANLII115/1995CANLII115.HTML

Bruni v. Bruni, 2010 ONSC 6568 (CanLII)—HTTPS://WWW.CANLII.ORG/EN/ON/ONSC/DOC/2010/2010ONSC6568/2010ONSC6568.HTML

Canadian Foundation for Children, Youth and the Law v. Canada (Attorney General), 2004 SCC 4 (CanLII)—HTTPS://WWW.CANLII.ORG/EN/CA/SCC/DOC/2004/2004SCC4/2004SCC4.HTML

Coates v. Watson, 2017 ONCJ 454 (CanLII)—HTTPS://WWW.CANLII.ORG/EN/ON/ONCJ/DOC/2017/2017ONCJ454/2017ONCJ454.HTML

Coates v. Watson, 2018 ONCJ 605 (CanLII)—HTTPS://WWW.CANLII.ORG/EN/ON/ONCJ/DOC/2018/2018ONCJ605/2018ONCJ605.HTML

Droit de la famille 081485, 2008 QCCS 2709 (CanLII)—HTTPS://WWW.CANLII.ORG/FR/QC/QCCS/DOC/2008/2008QCCS2709/2008QCCS2709.HTML

Eaton v. Brant County Board of Education, 1997 CanLII 366 (SCC)—HTTPS://WWW.CANLII.ORG/EN/CA/SCC/DOC/1997/1997CANLII366/1997CANLII366.HTML

Erazo v. Dufferin-Peel Catholic District School Board, 2014 ONSC 2072 (CanLII)—HTTPS://WWW.CANLII.ORG/EN/ON/ ONSC/DOC/2014/2014ONSC2072/2014ONSC2072.HTML

Gareau v. B.C. (Supt. of Fam. & Child Services), 1986 CanLII 1046 (BCSC)—HTTPS://WWW.CANLII.ORG/EN/BC/BCSC/ DOC/1986/1986CANLII1046/1986CANLII1046.HTML

Gillick v. West Norfolk & Wisbech Area Health Authority, [1985] 3 All E.R. 402 (H.L.)—HTTP://WWW.CIRP.ORG/LIBRARY/LEGAL/ UKLAW/GILLICKVWESTNORFOLK1985/

Haas v. Nyholm, 1923 CanLII 300 (SKQB)—HTTPS://WWW.CANLII. ORG/EN/SK/SKQB/DOC/1923/1923CANLII300/1923CANLII300.HTML

J.S.C. v. Wren, 1986 ABCA 249 (CanLII)—HTTPS://WWW.CANLII. ORG/EN/AB/ABCA/DOC/1986/1986ABCA249/1986ABCA249.HTML

L. (N.) v. M. (R.R.), 2016 ONSC 809 (CanLII)— HTTPS://WWW.CANLII.ORG/EN/ON/ONSC/DOC/2016/ 2016ONSC809/2016ONSC809.HTML

MacKinnon v. Harrison, 2011 ABCA 283 (CanLII)— HTTPS://WWW.CANLII.ORG/EN/AB/ABCA/DOC/2011/2011ABCA283/ 2011ABCA283.HTML

McDonald v. McDonald, 2017 BCCA 255 (CanLII)— HTTPS://WWW.CANLII.ORG/EN/BC/BCCA/DOC/2017/2017BCCA255/ 2017BCCA255.HTML

Multani v. Commission scolaire Marguerite-Bourgeoys, 2006 SCC 6 (CanLII)—HTTPS://WWW.CANLII.ORG/EN/CA/SCC/ DOC/2006/2006SCC6/2006SCC6.HTML

O.G. v. R.G., 2017 ONCJ 153 (CanLII)—HTTPS://WWW.CANLII.ORG/ EN/ON/ONCJ/DOC/2017/2017ONCJ153/2017ONCJ153.HTML

R. v. Barabash, 2015 SCC 29 (CanLII)—HTTPS://WWW.CANLII.ORG/ EN/CA/SCC/DOC/2015/2015SCC29/2015SCC29.HTML

R. v. Blake, 2003 BCCA 525 (CanLII)—HTTPS://WWW.CANLII.ORG/ EN/BC/BCCA/DOC/2003/2003BCCA525/2003BCCA525.HTML

R. v. C.M., 1995 Can LII 8924 (OCCA)—HTTPS://WWW.CANLII.ORG/EN/ON/ONCA/DOC/1995/1995CANLII8924/1995CANLII8924.HTML

R. v. M. (M.R.), 1998 CanLII 770 (SCC)—HTTPS://WWW.CANLII.ORG/EN/CA/SCC/DOC/1998/1998CANLII770/1998CANLII770.HTML

R. v. Morgentaler, 1988 CanLII 90 (SCC)—HTTPS://WWW.CANLII.ORG/EN/CA/SCC/DOC/1988/1988CANLII90/1988CANLII90.HTML

R. v. R.D., 2005 ABPC 54 (CanLII)—HTTPS://WWW.CANLII.ORG/EN/AB/ABPC/DOC/2005/2005ABPC54/2005ABPC54.HTML

R. v. Roth, 2002 ABQB 145 (CanLII)—HTTPS://WWW.CANLII.ORG/EN/AB/ABQB/DOC/2002/2002ABQB145/2002ABQB145.HTML

R. c. Roy, 1998 CanLII 12775 (QCCA)—HTTPS://WWW.CANLII.ORG/FR/QC/QCCA/DOC/1998/1998CANLII12775/1998CANLII12775.HTML

R. v. Sharpe, 2001 SCC 2 (CanLII)—HTTPS://WWW.CANLII.ORG/EN/CA/SCC/DOC/2001/2001SCC2/2001SCC2.HTML

R. v. T.C.F., 2006 NSCA 42 (CanLII)—HTTPS://WWW.CANLII.ORG/EN/NS/NSCA/DOC/2006/2006NSCA42/2006NSCA42.HTML

R.G. v. K.G., 2017 ONCA 108 (CanLII)—HTTPS://WWW.CANLII.ORG/EN/ON/ONCA/DOC/2017/2017ONCA108/2017ONCA108.HTML

S.L. v. Commission scolaire des Chênes, 2012 SCC 7 (CanLII)—HTTPS://WWW.CANLII.ORG/EN/CA/SCC/DOC/2012/2012SCC7/2012SCC7.HTML

Starson v. Swayze, 2003 SCC 32 (CanLII)—HTTPS://SCC-CSC.LEXUM.COM/SCC-CSC/SCC-CSC/EN/ITEM/2064/INDEX.DO

Young v. Young, 1993 CanLII 34 (SCC)—HTTPS://WWW.CANLII.ORG/EN/CA/SCC/DOC/1993/1993CANLII34/1993CANLII34.HTML

Zylberberg v. Sudbury Board of Education (Director), 1988 CanLII 189 (ONCA)—HTTPS://WWW.CANLII.ORG/EN/ON/ONCA/DOC/1988/1988CANLII189/1988CANLII189.HTML